Generosity
Rising

Other Books by Scott McKenzie
Climb Higher by Scott McKenzie and Kristine Miller
Bounty by Scott McKenzie and Kristine Miller

Generosity Rising

Lead a Stewardship Revolution in Your Church

Scott McKenzie

Abingdon Press
Nashville

GENEROSITY RISING:
LEAD A STEWARDSHIP REVOLUTION IN YOUR CHURCH

Copyright © 2016 by Abingdon Press

Library of Congress Cataloging-in-Publication Data has been requested.

ISBN 978-1-6308-8317-1

16 17 18 19 20 21 22 23 24 2–10 9 8 7 6 5 4 3 2 1
MANUFACTURED IN THE UNITED STATES OF AMERICA

Contents

Introduction

Don't remember the prior things; don't ponder ancient history. Look! I'm doing a new thing; now it sprouts up; don't you recognize it? I'm making a way in the desert, paths in the wilderness.

Isa 43:18-19 CEB

A Call to Revolution

There comes a time when the system no longer seems to work. When old processes become ineffective and standard operating procedures become obsolete. A time when revolution is the only viable option—a revolution that overthrows the old system and ushers in a new order. For the church, *now* is that time! Yes, you heard me right; the church today desperately needs a revolution in stewardship and generosity. The church today needs pastors and stewardship chairs willing to step forward and lead a revolution in generosity and giving.

Debbie's Story

Debbie came up to me prior to one of my stewardship workshops, "10 Keys to Unlocking the Secrets of Bountiful Generosity." Debbie's eyes were downcast and her face communicated discouragement, and I hadn't even started the workshop! She began to tell me how excited she was to be there but also how she was discouraged because she was the lone representative from her church. Debbie had tried to recruit others from her church, including her pastor, and gotten zero response. Debbie loves stewardship and lives a generous lifestyle. She believes effective stewardship changes lives and has the potential to radically change her church. Debbie knows changes are needed in her church around the issues of stewardship and giving, and she wanted to lead the revolution that would bring about change in her church. She was even willing to lead the charge, but when she looked back, no one was following. Debbie came and left alone.

Pastor Joe's Story

One day I received a voicemail from Pastor Joe, one of the finest pastors with whom I have ever worked. Pastor Joe had read all of the books and attended all of the workshops on stewardship. His church has a phenomenal ministry in a terribly blighted urban area. Their amazing ministries and missions change lives. But the church and leadership continually struggle with finances and stewardship. Some on the leadership team even fight, oppose, and sabotage efforts to increase stewardship and giving. And then Pastor Joe said this: "I just don't know what to do. I know the people who are fighting me don't give. What do I do? How do I change it?" He was willing to lead the charge for revolution that would bring change to his church, but he didn't know how to begin.

Steve's Story

Eight men gathered at a local restaurant for breakfast, prayer, and Bible study. Somehow the conversation turned to church giving and the issue of tithing. With profound sadness Steve said, "I tithe 10 percent to my church. I give an additional 8 percent to other Christian organizations. I find myself asking, why am I giving the 10 percent to the church? No one seems to ever come to Christ in our church. I don't see lives being changed. The other organizations are changing lives; why shouldn't I just give it all to them? What should I do?" Steve saw an ineffective system, and he was tired of it. Steve wanted to contribute where he could make an impact on people's lives. Steve wanted revolution.

My Story

What is your story? What prompted you to read this book? What concerns do you have about giving in your church?

We need revolution! The church needs people who are willing to step up and be revolutionary leaders. Do a search on stewardship and you will find nearly thirty-five hundred book titles on Amazon. Denominations of all sorts are offering stewardship and giving workshops on a regular basis. And yet, the Debbies of the world continue to be discouraged and frustrated as they stand alone and change never happens. Pastors like Pastor Joe become disillusioned when life-changing ministry goes unfunded and supposed leaders even oppose stewardship efforts to fund those ministries. People like Steve begin to wonder, why keep giving to an ineffective organization? Debbie, Pastor Joe, and Steve are not alone.

The State of Giving

The Empty Tomb, a research group focusing on giving in churches in the United States, reports in *The State of Church Giving through 2011* a decline in per-member giving for the fourth consecutive year. The Empty Tomb also reports that this four-year decline is the longest in their period of reporting such numbers, 1968–2011.[1] In fact, the only other longer period of decline was during the years of the Great Depression. Yes, you read that correctly; the only longer period of decline in giving occurred during the years of the Great Depression.

My State of Giving

What giving trends is your church experiencing?

The First Step

Why is this happening, and what can we do to reverse these disturbing trends? How can we bring about change, a revolution in hearts and behaviors? An answer just might be found in a grainy, jerky, homemade video apparently shot during the Sasquatch Music Festival in 2009. The video features a lone shirtless man in cutoffs dancing in an open field. Eventually, one person joins in the dance, then a second and third; in the end, an entire mob is dancing in the open field. In a TED Talk from February 2010, Derek Sivers uses this video to describe the making of a movement—in

---

1. Katherine Burgess, *Religion News Service*, "Report: Church Giving Reaches Depression-Era Record Lows," October 24, 2013.

other words, the making of a revolution. Here is an excerpt from Siver's TED Talk:

> The first follower transforms a lone nut into a leader. If the leader is the flint, the first follower is the spark that makes the fire. The second follower is a turning point: it's proof the first has done well. Now it's not a lone nut, and it's not two nuts. Three is a crowd, and a crowd is news. A movement must be public. Make sure outsiders see more than just the leader. Everyone needs to see the followers emulate followers, not the leader. Now here comes two more, then three more. Now we've got momentum. This is the tipping point! Now we've got a movement.[2]

My First Step
Take a few moments to watch this video: http://www.ted.com/talks/derek_sivers_how_to_start_a_movement

Generosity Rising

Pastors and stewardship chairs read the books, attend the workshops, and become lone nuts. They are stewardship versions of the dancing shirtless man; but too often no one joins them in the dance. And eventually, the lone nut quietly walks away, convinced she failed. This book is written for people who care about stewardship issues in their own lives and in the lives of their churches—the lone nuts who are passionate about stewardship and generosity. This book is about starting a movement, a revolution of generosity within our churches. It's a handbook on how to lead a revolution in generosity. I invite you on a journey, to go from being a lone nut to a revolutionary leader in generosity.

My Prayer for My Generosity Rising
Please write a sentence or two about what motivated you to read this book and what you pray will happen as a result. Use the space here or, preferably, keep a separate notebook or journal as you read through this book.

---

2. http://www.ted.com/talks/derek_sivers_how_to_start_a_movement.

We Hold These Truths...

He chose to give us birth by his true word, and here is the result: we are
like the first crop from the harvest of everything he created.

James 1:18 CEB

In considering how we might lead a revolution in generosity, let's look at one of the founding documents of the American Revolution, the Declaration of Independence. After a brief introduction, this brilliant document lays out the big picture, the big truth that will drive the revolution:

> We hold these truths to be a self-evident, that all men are created equal, and
> that they are endowed by their creator with certain unalienable rights, that
> among these are Life, Liberty and the pursuit of happiness.

Now that, my friends, is a cause worth fighting for; that big picture is one worth pursuing with all of one's heart, soul, and mind. Those words resonate so deeply with the human spirit that men and women throughout the course of our history have willingly paid the ultimate sacrifice. Throughout history, revolutions have always begun with a big picture and a cause worth fighting, and perhaps, dying for.

Before you recruit a single person to be on your stewardship team; before you begin your dance as the lone nut in the middle of the field; you need to know the big picture, the overarching cause, the big truth, that will drive this revolution of generosity.

Generosity Rising's Big Picture Is *Not*

First, let's look at what a revolution in generosity *will not* be about

- Raising larger sums of money from more people
- Getting more people to pledge or give
- Increasing the budget
- Paying the bills
- Paying the apportionments or denominational assessments
- Having a bigger, better building than the church next door or down the street
- Techniques or campaigns for raising money

Do any of the items listed above inspire you to revolution? Do any of the ideas above move you to sacrifice? Not me! And yet, don't those phrases describe much of what passes for stewardship in our churches?

Jane's Story

Jane was a generous contributor to her church. Jane lived and breathed stewardship. In August, her pastor came to her and asked her if she would be the stewardship chair for the following year. When she asked what it involved he responded, "We're in trouble, Jane. We need an 8 percent increase in giving to the budget or we will start to cut staff and probably not pay our denominational shares of ministry." The pastor continued, "When we get the line item budget finished you will stand in front of the congregation and present the budget and convince them that they need to give more. We will be able to show how much utility costs and our insurance premiums have gone up and also show that our staff has had no increase in three years. You let them know what will happen if they don't give more."

Jane replied to her pastor, "I'll get back to you." Jane finally sent an e-mail saying, "No thank you." Jane didn't want to die on that hill. Jane wanted to be part of a revolution. She wanted to be a part of a vital and life-changing movement in her church. Instead, she was offered a role in ongoing maintenance, business as usual. Jane wanted to inspire, but her pastor wanted to use fear and manipulation. Jane slowly drifted away from her church and finally left it completely. And guess what? Her money went with her. Jane, and so many people like her, want something more. Jane may not be able to name it, but what she wants is *a revolution in giving.*

Generosity Rising's Big Picture

Now, let's look at what a revolution in stewardship and giving must be about. Listen to the words of Tom Peters:

> Sometimes I think that all leadership literature stinks—including much of the stuff I've written. Too much focus is on tactics and motivation (and frankly, manipulation). All of that misses the point: leadership for what? From King and Gandhi and Jefferson...to Bill Gates and Steve Jobs and Richard Branson...leaders lead because they want to get some particular thing done. They want to do stuff that matters...great leaders are not merely great at leading. They are great at inducing others to take novel journeys to places of surpassing importance.[1]

Instead of looking for new tactics, new ways to manipulate, or new ways to make "the ask," Peters suggests that great leaders find and invite others to journey with them to a place of surpassing importance. So, let us start a revolution in stewardship and giving that leads to the place of surpassing importance and invite others to journey with us.

In the life of the church, what is the "stuff" that matters and where is the place of surpassing importance? What is the journey we are inviting people to? How will we inspire great leadership? Let us return to those words from the Declaration of Independence.

> We hold these truths to be a self-evident, that all men are created equal, and that they are endowed by their creator with certain unalienable rights, that among these are Life, Liberty and the pursuit of happiness.

These words penned by Thomas Jefferson in 1776 resonate with the words written by Tom Peters in 2006: "They want to do stuff that matters...great leaders are not merely great at leading. They are great at inducing others to take novel journeys to places of surpassing importance."

The revolution of giving and generosity has to be bigger than budgets, buildings, salaries, and denominational taxes. The revolution of giving and generosity has to be bigger than campaigns and tactics.

---

1. Tom Peters, *Reimagine: Business Excellence in a Disruptive Age* (New York: DK Publishing, 2006), 342.

3

I will now commit blasphemy and actually rewrite those amazing words in the Declaration of Independence because I believe they can help us find the place of surpassing importance for our revolution in generosity and giving:

> We hold these truths to be self-evident that all people are created in the image of a loving, giving, and generous God. We believe real life, true liberty, and eternal joy are only realized when we live lives of abundant generosity and sacrificial love.

The big picture, the big cause, the place of surpassing importance for a revolution in generosity is nothing short of enabling individuals to become the very people God created them to be. What a novel journey of surpassing importance: the journey of becoming the person God created me to be from the beginning of all creation. Now that, my friends, is what a revolution in generosity is all about.

George's Story

George is a former fighter pilot who flew several missions during the Vietnam War. I was returning to work another capital campaign with George's church, and in the midst of talking about our previous campaign George said, "What we did during that last campaign was the single most transformative experience of my life." How was a capital campaign the single most transformative experience in George's life? The campaign was essentially an invitation to go on the journey of becoming the person God created George to be from the beginning of creation. Our place of surpassing importance was not a building project. Our place of surpassing importance was to be the people God created us to be. And unlike Jane, George is now committed to being part of a revolution in his church, a revolution in generosity.

Your Story

Let's return to the words written on the very first page.

Before you recruit a single person to be on your stewardship team, before you begin your dance as the lone nut in the middle of the field, you need to know the big picture—the overarching cause, the big truth—that will drive this revolution of generosity. If you get this part wrong, the revolution will fail and like many failed revolutionaries you just might end up in exile or worse! A revolution in generosity *will not* be about

- Raising larger sums of money from more people
- Getting more people to pledge or give
- Increasing the budget
- Paying the bills
- Paying the apportionments or denominational assessments
- Having a bigger, better building than the church next door or down the street
- Techniques or campaigns for raising money

Stop right now and answer some very fundamental questions:

- Is my current vision of stewardship and generosity about changing lives or about maintaining the church budget? Be honest!
- Will my vision of stewardship and generosity change the world or just keep the doors open?
- Is my current vision of stewardship and generosity a hill worth dying on?
- Do I view stewardship as primarily about tactics and campaigns or as a life-changing journey of surpassing importance?

Name the Enemy

Yes, every revolution needs a cause, the big picture, a vision for a new way of life; but revolutions also need an enemy. For example, immediately after painting a picture of life, liberty, and the pursuit of happiness, Thomas Jefferson goes on to describe the enemy of this new reality, and he uses phrases like "absolute despotism" and "absolute tyranny."

The history of the present King of Great Britain is a history of repeated injuries and usurpations, all having in direct object the establishment of absolute tyranny over these States. To prove this, let Facts be submitted to a candid world.

Jefferson then lists twenty-seven examples of these "injuries and usurpations."

5

Mike Figliuolo at thoughtLEADERS, LLC wrote an article entitled "Everyone Needs a Little Revolution." In the article, Figliuolo writes,

> Revolution is that point in time when a critical mass of people get fed up with some kind of crap and collectively decide to do something about it. That something is usually scary, somewhat extreme, painful, brave, and life altering.[2]

I realize that many are cringing; some may even be offended at some of the language he uses. The truth is, it fits, and is wonderfully descriptive of what seems to be happening in many churches all across America. And just maybe it is time for us to be offended and fed up with the many deficiencies in the arena of stewardship, giving, and generosity. In the words of Thomas Jefferson, "To prove this let Facts be submitted to a candid world." Here are the facts on stewardship, giving, and generosity in the United States:

- Episcopalians give 2% to charities—55% of that 2% goes to religion (church) for a total of 1.1%.
- Presbyterians give 1.8% to charities—53.9% of that 1.8% goes to religion (church) for a total of 1.0%.
- Lutherans give 1.7% to charities—61.8% of that 1.7% goes to religion (church) for a total of 1.1%.
- Methodists give 1.6% to charities—61.5% of that 1.6% goes to religion (church) for a total of 1%.
- Catholics give 1.5% to charities—50.7% of that 1.5% goes to religion (church) for a total of .8%.[3]
- From 1987 to 2013 giving to religion as a percent of total charitable giving has declined from 52% to 31%.[4]
- From 2012 to 2013 charitable giving increased by 4.4%. Giving to religion as a subset declined by 0.2%.[5]

2. www.thoughtleadersllc.com/2011/10/everyone-needs-a-little-revolution/.
3. Patrick Rooney, "Dispelling Common Beliefs about Giving to Religious Institutions in the United States," in *Religious Giving: For Love of God*, ed. David H. Smith (Bloomington: Indiana University Press, 2010), 5.
4. *Giving USA 2015: Annual Report on Philanthropy for the year 2014* (Bloomington: Lilly School of Philanthropy, Indiana University, 2015), 17.
5. Ibid.

In 2010, I conducted two capital campaigns. One was located in an economically depressed urban area with considerably high unemployment and an extremely high rate of incarceration for males. The other was in a wealthy suburban area often touted as one of the ten best places to live in America. The giving statistics were amazingly similar; both had over 35 percent of their active giving families giving less than three hundred dollars annually. For the rich white suburbanites, that should be a huge concern and a call to action. Most refused to see it that way, however. In fact, when forced to acknowledge this reality, they gave reasons and excuses why the situation is perfectly acceptable. After all...

- We have high levels of income but our cost of living is high.
- Yes, we could give more but we have two children we are going to need to put through college.
- Well, you know the economy has hit us hard as well. People just can't afford to give.

Where is the offense and outrage? Where is the revolutionary leader willing to stand up, face the enemy, and say, "This is wrong. This has to change"?

A Pastor's Story

A pastor called the other day and said he was having trouble with his finance committee. They refused to talk about stewardship and refused to ask people to step up their giving. Their solution to the church's financial difficulties was to cut the budget. Where can we cut? They recently spent an hour discussing the pluses and minuses of cutting postage by just handing newsletters out after worship. And then he used the line I hear all the time, "We don't want to offend anyone. Our people are giving all they can." *No!* Let's stand up and face our enemy. Our people are giving all they want to give. The pastor then made the most revealing statement of all: "Very few of the members of the finance team are generous givers." Of course they want to cut the budget; they don't want to give more. Our people love stuff more than God. Our people love money more than they love Jesus. There, my friends, is the enemy.

Naming Your Enemy

Just as the American Revolution required the big picture and a naming of the enemy, the same is true for a real revolution in generosity and giving.

This is nothing new. Jesus knew the power of giving to transform lives but he also knew the power of money and love of stuff to draw us away from God.

And so I end this chapter with a devotion based on a poignant and profound story from the Gospels, the story of the rich young ruler or rich young man. I invite you to read it slowly and prayerfully. Hear the story again: "Jesus looked at him carefully and loved him. He said, 'You are lacking one thing. Go, sell what you own, and give the money to the poor. Then you will have treasure in heaven. And come, follow me.' But the man was dismayed at this statement and went away saddened, because he had many possessions" (Mark 10:21-22 CEB).

Jesus looked him hard in the eye—and loved him! How often do we think Jesus really just loves the poor, the sick, and the downtrodden? Of course Jesus loves the poor, the sick, and the downtrodden. Jesus also has a very special place in his heart for those with resources, and yes, even those with wealth. Jesus wants those with wealth and resources to know him, love him, and follow him. Jesus knows that this young man is so close to becoming the unique creation God intended him to be from the beginning of time. But Jesus also knows the enemy: love of stuff and love of money.

So Jesus confronts the enemy head on and says, "Go, sell what you own, and give the money to the poor." Jesus asks, "What do you love more than me?" For this young man the answer was clear: he loved stuff, money, and wealth more than Jesus. And so the young man turned away. And Jesus let him go. Can you imagine this scene in your head? "But the man was dismayed at this statement and went away saddened, because he had many possessions."

Jesus looks us hard in the eye, and with a heart overflowing with love, he asks, "What do you love more than me?" What are you holding on tight to and not about to let go? For a mother or father it could be children. For someone else it could be a parent or even a spouse. For others the answer may be found in a job, a career, or a home. For many of us it may very well be our wealth and our stuff. Maybe it's the sense of pride and accomplishment that comes with having wealth and all the right "stuff." Maybe it's something very different like anger, bitterness, or an unwillingness to forgive that we refuse to let go. Jesus stands in front of us, looks us hard in the eye with love, and asks, "What do you love more than me?"

- Am I willing to be the kind of revolutionary leader exemplified by Jesus?

8

- Do I really believe in the glorious vision of people living in the image of our all-loving and all-generous creator?

- Do I believe we are created to be giving and generous?

- Am I fed up with the levels of giving and all the excuses people, myself included, make to not give?

- Am I willing to name the enemy and ask the Jesus question, "What do you love more than me?"

- Am I willing, like Jesus, to let people walk away when they choose stuff over God?

God, I want to love you with all my heart. But there always seems to be stuff that gets in the way. Help me now to let go, to release whatever my stuff is to you, your love, and your care. God, I want to be a revolutionary leader. I want to walk with people on this amazing journey of generosity as we become more and more like you. Amen.

Becoming a Revolutionary Leader and Team

You are the light of the world. A city on top of a hill can't be hidden.

Matt 5:14 CEB

We have identified our place of surpassing importance for the revolution, the big picture, the cause worth fighting for...

We hold these truths to be self-evident that all people are created in the image of a loving, giving, and generous God. We believe real life, true liberty, and eternal joy are only realized when we live lives of abundant generosity and sacrificial love.

We have identified the enemy, the truth that most of our people are not giving generously. We have heard discussions around the finance table about the need to cut expenses rather than increase our own giving. We are not giving all we can and most of us love our stuff more than Jesus!

Becoming a Revolutionary Leader

So what is next? If you want to lead a revolution in generosity you better be living a revolutionary lifestyle. Nothing will kill a revolution in generosity quicker than a leader who doesn't practice and live the principles of the revolution. When I begin working with a church in stewardship, the first indicator of success will be, where is the pastor's name on the giving list? The second indicator is, where is the finance or stewardship chair's name on the giving list? If their names are nowhere to be found or are near the bottom, we will in all likelihood fail to bring about a true revolution in generosity. Oh, we may raise money, but there will be no enduring revolution.

The Core Strategy Group, led by Scott Miller and David Morey, posted an online article entitled "How to Lead a Revolution."[1] This think tank advises corporations and political leaders in the art of revolution and insurgency. They state that if a person wants to make change, to lead a revolution, that person must intentionally live the intended outcome him- or herself. There will be no revolution in generosity if you are not living, practicing, and demonstrating generosity. Stop now to pray and reflect on these questions.

- As I look at the way I live and give, am I a reflection of the revolution I want to see happen in my church?
- Am I content with what I give or am I striving to always find ways to give more?
- Where am I on the giving list and does that position reflect real leadership?

Becoming a Revolutionary Team

Leading a revolution in generosity requires living a revolution in generosity. But unless you want to be the shirtless man dancing in the middle of the field all alone, you need to begin recruiting like-minded revolutionaries. You will be simply a nut, a lone nut, until people begin to join in the dance. In the words of Derek Sivers: "The first follower transforms a lone nut into a leader.... The second follower is a turning point: it's proof the first has done well. Now it's not a lone nut, and it's not two nuts. Three is a crowd and a crowd is news."[2]

People often ask for my perspective on what makes a stewardship campaign, or capital campaign, successful. They want to know how it is possible to raise so much money. The answer is always the same: with the right leadership team, nothing will stop us from being successful. So of course the next question is, what makes for a good leadership team?

---

1. Corestrategygroup.com, May 17, 2011.
2. Derek Sivers, TED Talk, February 2010, http://www.ted.com/talks/derek
_sivers_how_to_start_a_movement.

Who to Recruit?

Let me answer the question with a story. When doing a feasibility study in a large and growing suburban church the pastor pulled me aside and said, "The next person you interview is the one I have tapped to be the campaign chair. He is president and founder of his own company and he gives away lots of money." So I watched with eager anticipation as he pulled into the parking lot in his brand-new Mercedes. His beautiful suit appeared to have been custom tailored. After brief introductions he then said, "I really don't believe in the project and I plan on just giving a token gift of five thousand dollars." He then went on to say, "I give to my university and am chairing their capital campaign." We finished the survey and he left.

The next person to be interviewed arrived in a used car at least ten years old. Her clothes were neat and appropriate, but clearly not meant to impress anyone. She sat down, and before I could even introduce myself she said, "I just love my church. When my husband died two years ago my church surrounded me with love and care. I couldn't have survived without my pastor and my church." Then we began to talk about her possible gift. She told me about her late husband who was a teacher and loved anything to do with children and youth. She then said, "Now I'm not rich but I am comfortable. My husband had a life insurance policy worth lots of money. I'd like to use that money and be the lead giver to our family life center and youth building."

If you asked the average person to review these two candidates on paper and then decide who should be recruited to be on your financial leadership team, almost everyone would choose the successful businessperson. And of course, they would be wrong. In my experience, finance and stewardship teams are typically made up of people with some kind of background in finances: bankers, CPAs, personal financial planners, investors, and so forth. If not involved in the financial industry, we often look to people who run successful businesses. While these people can be wonderful and productive members of a stewardship team, a background in finances or running a successful business is not the number one criterion for being on the team.

The number one criterion for being a part of the stewardship or finance team is a demonstrated history of generous giving to the church. In other words, if you want to lead a revolution, you better surround yourself with other revolutionaries. Who else believes in the cause and who else knows the enemy and is willing to go to battle? Is there anyone else who takes offense and is outraged at so many people giving such small amounts to the church? Find them and make them part of the team. Bottom line, you need to pick your leaders carefully and they need to be people with a demonstrated track record of generosity and sacrificial giving. This does not mean that your chosen leaders need to be the largest contributors to your church but their giving needs to represent a meaningful and substantial commitment relative to their means. So here we have an important distinction between leading a revolution in generosity and our shirtless dancing man. Our shirtless dancing man was content to have anyone join the movement, even as a first or second follower. Allowing just anyone to help lead your revolution in generosity will almost surely lead to failure. A young pastor came up to me after a workshop and said how much she agreed with everything that was said. She said, "I am that lone nut. But I know I need a team and so I put a blurb in the bulletin and newsletter asking anyone interested in stewardship to join me." Her revolution will fail. Moving from a lone nut to a revolutionary leader requires intentional recruitment of fellow believers in the cause.

Steps for Recruiting Revolutionary Leaders

1. Gather Information That Helps Make Your Case

Recruitment of fellow revolutionaries requires accurate information. If you are going to lead a real revolution in generosity you need to know who gives generously. You cannot make blind guesses or assumptions about who gives generously. You need good information.

Whenever I do a feasibility study for a campaign, a significant part of the study is an analysis of giving patterns. Typically, I ask the church to fill out a form similar to the chart below. I have filled in this form with numbers from an actual church.

Number of Giving Households	Giving Level	Total Given by Households in Range
1	$15,000 or Above	$16,700
9	$10,000–$14,999	$100,466
18	$6,000–$9,999	$134,719
50	$3,000–$5,999	$216,281
31	$2,000–$2,999	$76,279
21	$1,500–$1,999	$35,650

28	$1,000–$1,499	$33.543
49	$500–$999	$35,851
19	$300–$499	$7,968
87	Less than $300	$8,398
Total Number of Giving Households = 313		Total Dollars Given = $665,855

Looking at these numbers we see

- Only 25 percent of the families contribute over 70 percent of all dollars.
- Roughly one-third (34 percent) of all giving families give less than $500.00.
- It is important to know that the average household income in this area is over $64,000.00.

There are often two responses when I present this information. One group will express outrage and another group will immediately begin to make excuses about why this is acceptable in their particular church and community. Guess whom I will ask to join the revolution? Remember, a successful revolution requires a group of people who know the place of surpassing importance and are willing to face the enemy. They are willing to take offense to, and express outrage about, the current levels of giving to the church.

2. Know the Actual Giving List

Yes, this is really a subset of accurate information but this particular point can be so controversial that it requires its own emphasis. In my experience there are typically two groups or persons responsible for wanting to keep the giving list secret: entrenched nongiving leadership and, surprisingly, the pastor. Let's consider the opposition of entrenched nongiving leadership. When a person knows his or her name is not on the giving list, do you really think they want the pastor to know the list? No! Most of us prefer our sins remain in the dark. Recently, one of my churches was considering a special thank-you to people who had demonstrated commitment and generosity over the previous year. Leadership received a scathing e-mail from a church member. The church member used several telling phrases. "Nobody's giving should be singled out for thanks because all giving is equal in the eyes of God." "All of us are giving what we can." Because I had the giving lists, I immediately checked, and guess what, the author's name was nowhere to be found on the giving list. How do we deal with entrenched nongiving leadership when we are trying to start a revolution in generosity? Remind yourself of the stakes involved. You will need to once again decide, do you really believe in the fundamental truth of this revolution?

> We hold these truths to be self-evident that all people are created in the image of a loving, giving and generous God. We believe real life, true liberty and eternal joy are only realized when we live lives of abundant generosity and sacrificial love.

If you believe this, then for the good of the individual as well as the church you need to have an honest discussion about what it means to be a disciple, what it means to be a member of the church, and what it means to be a leader. Wouldn't we want to give a person a chance to grow in this way, to fully embrace what it means to be living as a disciple? Remember, people don't like their sin to be brought into the light and you must be prepared for people to quit and leave. If you recall, Jesus didn't go running after the rich young man in Mark 10. He didn't say, "Wait, I really didn't mean all that stuff about giving." Jesus let him go.

The second group or person who may oppose knowing the giving list is the pastor. In my experience there are two basic reasons why pastors may not want to see the giving list. One, they know that their name is not on it. Bob graduated from seminary with significant debt and had talked himself into believing that he didn't need to financially support the church because he wasn't making as much as he could in the "real world." Bob didn't want to see the giving list because he knew in his heart he was wrong. After attending a workshop on giving Bob stood in front of his congregation and told his story. He admitted he was wrong and told them he and his wife were going to begin immediately giving 5 percent with the goal of being at a full tithe in two years. Bob challenged other leaders and church members to join him and his wife. Bob's willingness to look at his own giving allowed him the courage to ask for and look at the giving list.

The second reason some clergy don't want to know the giving list is their fear that they will not be able to handle the information in an appropriate manner. If you do not believe you can be trusted with this information, then you should have serious questions about your fitness for this vocation. If you cannot be trusted with knowing what people give, how can you be trusted with issues of marital fidelity or infidelity, addiction, abuse, or any one of a hundred issues faced by our people in the pews? What do you do if the leaders absolutely refuse to give you access to the giving records? Brenda became convinced that knowing the giving list was imperative if she was going to have a chance at leading a revolution in generosity. Simply demanding the list ended up with a stalemate. Brenda decided to go a bit more slowly and in steps. She put together a stair step chart popularized by Herb Miller's *The New Consecration Sunday.*

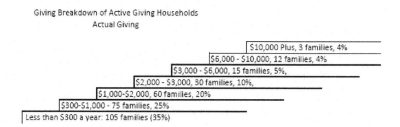

Giving Breakdown of Active Giving Households
Actual Giving

$10,000 Plus, 3 families, 4%
$6,000 - $10,000, 12 families, 4%
$3,000 - $6,000, 15 families, 5%,
$2,000 - $3,000, 30 families, 10%,
$1,000-$2,000, 60 families, 20%
$300-$1,000 - 75 families, 25%
Less than $300 a year: 105 families (35%)

The stair step chart showed that 35 percent of all actual giving units in her church gave less than three hundred dollars. The chart then showed how many families gave at various step levels all the way to the top to those families giving over ten thousand dollars. Brenda found that three families were giving 20 percent of the budget. Brenda went with this information to her board and shared her concern about the large percentage of families giving less than three hundred dollars. She explained this was a spiritual problem that needed to be addressed with love and concern but she couldn't without the giving list. She also explained that having three families give 20 percent of the budget put the church in a precarious position and suggested that the board consider inviting those donors to look at planned giving but again could not without the list. In the end, the board refused the total list, but they did agree to let her see names on the various steps in alphabetical order.

One year after Brenda was given this initial information, people realized she was not using the information inappropriately and she was given access to the entire list. In a fascinating twist, after Brenda left and the new pastor came in, church leaders just assumed the new pastor would have access to the giving records. Get what you can get, maybe the top twenty givers in alphabetical order without amounts, and eventually you will have the entire giving list.

A word of warning—knowing the giving list leads to incredible joy and inspiration. Knowing the giving list leads to great sadness and frustration. You will look at the list and see the true widow's mite giver and you will be blessed. You will see people who have multiple luxury cars, multiple homes, kids in private colleges and their name is nowhere to be found on the giving list. You will be sad and angry.

3. Have a Job Description When You Recruit

You have gathered information and reviewed the giving list. You are ready to recruit your fellow revolutionary leaders. So what's next in choosing those who will fight beside you in this revolution of generosity? Remember Tom Peter's quote on leadership: "They want to do stuff that matters . . . great leaders are not merely great at 'leading.' They are great at inducing others to take on novel journeys to places of surpassing importance."[3]

As you prepare to invite people to join in your revolution, remind yourself of the big picture. Remind yourself that you are inviting people on a journey to a place of lasting and even eternal importance.

> We hold these truths to be self-evident that all people are created in the image of a loving, giving, and generous God. We believe real life, true liberty, and eternal joy are only realized when we live lives of abundant generosity and sacrificial love.

You are *not* recruiting people to raise money for the annual budget. You are *not* asking people to ask others for money. You are inviting people to join you in helping people to find that place of surpassing importance. You are asking people to join you in

- Helping people discover their deepest identity as created in the image of a loving and generous God
- Helping people experience true liberty and eternal joy through abundant generosity and sacrificial love

---

3. Tom Peters, *Re-imagine: Business Excellence in a Disruptive Age* (New York: DK Publishing, 2006), 342.

And that, my friends, is the "stuff that matters"! This is way too important to simply put an announcement in the bulletin and ask for volunteers. This is way too important to simply say, "Oh, all you have to do is come to a few meetings. This isn't a big deal." As Miller and McKenzie said in *Climb Higher*, "If we tell prospective committee members that their role isn't as big as they imagine, the time commitment is less than they think, and they can probably miss about half the meetings and still serve, what does that say about the importance of the role they are being asked to fulfill?"[4]

Yes, this is a big deal! Because this is a big deal, you need to have a job description for the stewardship and generosity team. People need a clear understanding of the importance and significance of this job. Here is a sample job description you can modify and share with your potential team members.

Job Description for Stewardship and Generosity

We Believe: all people are created in the image of a loving, giving, and generous God. We believe all we have is a gift from God and real life, true liberty, and eternal joy are only realized when we live lives of abundant generosity and sacrificial love.

Who: Stewardship team members should be people who

- Are mature in both their relationship to Christ and have a demonstrated history of generous giving
- Are committed to the mission and vision of the church and are regular in attendance and participate in other activities
- Are willing to share the joy of giving/tithing with others
- Are tithing or committed to working toward a tithe

What: Responsibilities of the stewardship team include but are not limited to

- Study and growth in your personal understanding of biblical stewardship, encouraging others to do the same

---

4. Scott McKenzie and Kristine Miller, *Climb Higher* (Nashville: Abingdon Press, 2011), 29.

- Planning a year-round stewardship program
- Demonstrating on a regular basis how money and finances help accomplish the mission and vision of the church
- Regularly telling stories of how lives are being changed by ministry
- Making sure that at some point all age groups are engaged in some stewardship study
- Making sure new members are invited to begin the stewardship journey
- Planning multiple and creative ways of saying thank you to those who give
- Building into church life opportunities for people to express gratitude to God
- Building intentional prayer time into any and all stewardship efforts, continually asking, "Lord, what do you want to do through me?"
- Intentionally looking for people who have stepped up their giving and encouraging them to tell their story

Pay and Benefits: You will know the joy of having made a significant and life-changing difference in your church and individuals within your church. You have been part of a life-changing revolution!

Your Stewardship Team

People reading this chapter may be tempted to think that I am encouraging stacking a stewardship team with "big givers." Not so. *I am encouraging churches to stack the stewardship team with people who passionately believe in both their church and in giving to their church.* So I end this chapter with a devotion describing the kinds of persons we want on the stewardship team.

While they were being tested by many problems, their extra amount of happiness and their extreme poverty resulted in a surplus of rich generosity. I assure you that they gave what they could afford and even more than they could afford, and they did it voluntarily. They urgently begged us for the privilege of sharing in this service for the saints. They even exceeded our expectations, because they gave themselves to the Lord first and to us, consistent with God's will. (2 Cor 8:2-5 CEB)

One of the blessings of my job is I occasionally encounter one of the true saints of the church. While doing interviews in a very economically depressed area suffering from severe unemployment and all the problems associated with poverty, I met Miss Charlotte. Miss Charlotte came into the room with what appeared to be a slight limp, and when she spoke she slurred certain words. My thought was, she is suffering the aftereffects of a stroke. When we talked about her possibility of giving to a capital campaign, she responded she was unable to because she had been the victim of a financial scam, had lost a large sum of money, and was forced into bankruptcy. But then her eyes lit up and a calm, beautiful smile came across her face as she then said, "But I haven't reduced my tithe. I asked the court permission to continue my giving to the church." Then she continued, "When I get out of bankruptcy in three years then I will be able to give something to the capital campaign." She ended our conversation by saying, "God has been so good to me. He has given me everything I have. He continues to care for me and I have everything I need because of him." Truly, I was in the presence of one of the true saints of God.

> Oh God, help me to trust you like Miss Charlotte does. Forgive me for my lack of trust and my worries about the future. Give me a spirit of gratitude and a heart for generosity, even when it seems to make no sense. Amen.

- When I make choices about finances and giving, do I operate from a spirit of fear or trust?

- Can I recall a time when, like Miss Charlotte, I gave generously and it really didn't make financial sense? What happened?

Give me a stewardship team made up of Miss Charlottes and generosity will rise and the revolution will be won!

Generosity Boot Camp

*Don't be conformed to the patterns of this world, but be transformed by
the renewing of your minds so that you can figure out what God's will
is—what is good and pleasing and mature.*

Rom 12:2 CEB

We have identified the big picture, the big truth driving our generosity revolution:

We hold these truths to be self-evident that all people are created
in the image of a loving, giving, and generous God. We believe real life,
true liberty, and eternal joy are only realized when we live lives of abundant
generosity and sacrificial love.

Then, we recruited people with a track record of demonstrated generosity to
be part of our generosity team. What's next? We need to train the generosity team. You might think it's sufficient to simply pull everybody together
for an initial meeting and pass out job descriptions. No! Remember, we are
talking nothing short of a revolution in generosity, and that requires new
ways of thinking, living, and in fact, being. The invitation to be part of the
generosity team is not an invitation to be part of a committee but to be a
part of a revolution.

Generosity Boot Camp

We need a generosity boot camp. Do a Google search on *what is the
purpose of boot camp* and you will discover some very interesting answers
and anecdotes. Jon Davis, a marine sergeant and Iraq war veteran, responds
to the following question on the website Quora: *What is the logic behind*

making military boot camps intensive? Mr. Davis states, "You have to train 18-year-olds to run to the sound of gunfire and perform under fire and the threat of death. This act defies all logic, goes against all human instinct, and takes one of the most intensive acts of psychological reprogramming to overcome."[1]

One could argue that the purpose of boot camp is conversion, a changing of the heart. In our culture, living a life of abundant generosity and sacrificial giving "defies all logic." Think about it: "You want me to give away significant amounts of *my* money, money I have earned?" I would certainly say such a request defies logic, at least the logic of our culture. Abundant generosity and sacrificial giving requires a conversion of heart, mind, and pocketbook. In *The Spirituality of Fundraising*, Henri Nouwen states, "Fund-raising is also always a call to conversion.... To be converted means to experience a deep shift in how we see and think and act. Fund-raising as ministry involves a real conversion."[2]

The church today desperately needs a generosity boot camp, a place where our *recruits* experience conversion! A great place to begin training for the generosity team is an overnight retreat. We are not talking twelve weeks like the Marine Corps, just an overnight retreat. Believe me, I understand there will be considerable resistance. People will insist they don't have the time to spare and will try to turn an overnight retreat into an hour-and-a-half-long committee meeting. Stand firm and remember, we are talking about revolution and conversion. One of the first decisions will be location. I strongly encourage you to go off-site at a local or denominational retreat center. Getting people away from the routine of life, even if just overnight, creates openness to change and conversion.

What happens at this retreat? Generosity boot camp accomplishes three specific tasks:

- Confronting and dumping our money baggage
- Learning the three core values of our revolution
- Creating a personal and group generosity declaration

We will examine each of these specific tasks and then end this chapter with a suggested retreat outline.

---

1. www.quora.com/What-is-the-logic-behind-making-military-bootcamps-intensive.

2. Henri Nouwen, *The Spirituality of Fundraising*, ed. John S. Mogabgab (Nashville: Upper Room, 2010), 4.

Confronting and Dumping
Our Money Baggage

Imagine for a moment raw marine recruits stepping off the bus, thrust into formation, marching off to get the Marine Corps haircut, surrendering their clothes and their possessions. Clearly, the recruits leave the old way of life at home as they begin the process of becoming marines. Joining and leading the generosity revolution requires a very similar process, with, of course, a very different methodology! Stewardship recruits need to examine their personal relationship with money and confront the truth of money's place in one's life. Nouwen says it this way: "Those of us who ask for money need to look carefully at ourselves. The question is not how to get money. Rather, the question is about our relationship with money. We will never be able to ask for money if we do not know how we ourselves relate to money. What is the place of money in our lives?"[3]

All of us have baggage regarding the importance and place of money in our lives. When I conduct a feasibility study prior to a capital campaign, people often share very openly their money baggage and their stories about how they came to pick up their baggage. In discussing a possible gift one older man spoke eloquently about the pain of watching a grandfather die penniless in a county nursing home. He remembers saying to himself, "That will never happen to me." All of his adult life he has saved and scrimped. Generosity does not come easily because of the fear that he will end up like his grandfather. This gentleman truly wants to be part of the revolution but struggles with his money baggage and will never fully embrace the revolution until he examines, in the words of Nouwen, his "relationship with money."

A young man in his early thirties told me how he came to be a tither. The journey was not an easy one. John grew up in what he described as a working poor neighborhood. When John became a teenager and began to work part-time he wanted only one thing, a Chevy Camaro. After getting married and starting a family John began to earn decent money and his first purchase was a Chevy Camaro. He knew he couldn't afford the payments or upkeep for this car. He knew it wasn't a smart decision, but in his words, he "had to have it." John became involved in a local church and with the encouragement of his pastor, John and his wife participated in David Ramsey's Financial Peace University, a kind of financial boot camp.

John will tell anyone who listens that dealing with his money baggage changed his life. John came to understand that his beloved Camaro did not

---

3. Ibid., 11.

mean he was a success or a "real man." John wanted to become a giver and a tither but could not as long as he had the Camaro. With a wry smile John now talks about the joy of giving and being generous while driving a used mini-van with over one hundred thousand miles.

All of us carry some kind of money baggage. One way to help identify and then dump the baggage is through the use of a money autobiography. Prior to your retreat/boot camp send your potential revolutionaries a list of the following questions:

- What is your earliest memory about money? Can you recall a happy childhood memory involving money? Are there any unhappy memories involving money from your childhood?
- Did you feel poor or wealthy while growing up? Would you describe your childhood as one of abundance or scarcity?
- Describe your parents' attitudes toward money.
- When did you first have your "own" money? Were you taught anything about how to handle your "first" money?
- How do you feel about your current financial status, and does it affect your self-esteem?
- Do you worry excessively about money?
- Would you describe yourself as a generous giver, a careful giver, or a very frugal giver?

There are several versions of a money autobiography available. The Episcopal Network for Stewardship offers one on their website at http://tens.org.

After your recruits have gathered and become acquainted, spend time in groups of two or three sharing responses to the above questions. Encourage open and honest dialogue by sharing some of your personal money autobiography. Bring the entire group back together for a large group discussion. Only when we acknowledge the importance and influence of money in our own lives can we make a deliberate and conscious choice to join the generosity revolution. We name our baggage, we claim our baggage, and then we can dump our money baggage.

The Three Core Values of the Revolution

After the naming, claiming, and dumping of money baggage, the next task in your leaders' retreat is the teaching of generosity core values. Just as marine recruits are taught the core values of honor, courage, and commitment, generosity recruits need to be taught the core values of generosity:

gratitude, prayer, and faith. "Stewardship is grounded in gratitude, revealed in prayer, and lived in faith."[4]

Gratitude—Everything a Gift

Gratitude flows from the recognition that who we are and what we have are gifts and what we have are gifts to be received and shared. Gratitude releases us from the bonds of obligation and prepares us to offer ourselves freely and fully for the work of the Kingdom.[5]

We will never embrace a revolution of generosity until we recognize the basic truth that everything we have and all that we are comes from the hand of God as a gift. Conversely, when everything I have is the product of my own initiative and my own work, why would I be generous and giving?

Diane's Gratitude Story

Diane was the poster child for the self-made woman. Her mother suffered from alcoholism and she never knew her father. Diane basically raised herself. As a teenager Diane worked multiple jobs just to keep food on the table for herself and her mother. Studying at night, Diane eventually became a licensed real estate agent and by the age of forty owned her own agency. Diane owned multiple homes and drove cars that cost more than other peoples' homes. Diane described herself as a token giver; after all, if she made it on her own, anybody could.

Then came the day that would forever change Diane's life. Diane discovered a lump on her breast. Doctors told Diane the cancer was advanced and aggressive. For the first time in her life, Diane stood toe-to-toe with an opponent that could not be overcome with hard work and determination. Eventually, with the prayerful support of her church family, the tireless efforts of her doctors, and, according to Diane, the healing touch of God's hand, Diane beat cancer. Diane continues to be an incredibly successful real estate agent.

At her church's generosity boot camp Diane tells the group how cancer and then gratitude forever changed her life. Diane now believes in her heart that all she has and all she is is a gift "to be received and shared." Gratitude

---

4. Scott McKenzie and Kristine Miller, *Climb Higher* (Nashville: Abingdon Press, 2011), 41.

5. Nouwen, *The Spirituality of Fundraising*, 35

set Diane free from the burden of being a self-made woman and now Diane offers herself "freely and fully for the work of the Kingdom." Diane now sponsors a shelter for homeless mothers with children. Every Friday, you can find Diane working at the shelter; and if you ask her why, her answer would be one simple word—gratitude.

Obviously there are numerous scripture references regarding gratitude. Before doing a mini-Bible study on gratitude during boot camp, invite your recruits to reflect on some fundamental questions and assumptions about gratitude. Find and invite someone like Diane to share his or her story. If you do not have a Diane in your group then find one in your congregation and have their story videotaped. If you cannot come up with anyone, consider the video clip at www.karmatube.org/videos.php?id=3008. The video tells the inspiring story of Alice Herz Sommer. At age 108, Alice, who survived the concentration camps and later cancer at the age of eighty-three, says her most important lesson in life is "to be thankful for everything... for sun and a smile... everything is a present... this I learned, to be thankful for everything."

Invite your generosity boot camp recruits to go off by themselves and reflect on the video or witness. Then invite them to consider the following devotion: "Brothers and sisters, we want to let you know about the grace of God that was given to the churches of Macedonia. While they were being tested by many problems, their extra amount of happiness and their extreme poverty resulted in a surplus of rich generosity" (2 Cor 8:1-2 CEB).

Sasha's Gratitude Story

Sasha is a ten-year-old Russian orphan. When my church group visited, Sasha, for some reason, latched on to me. He took me by the arm and led me through the orphanage showing off his room and the place he ate meals. All the while Sasha's eyes were filled with joy and laughter. In spite of the fact that I spoke little Russian and Sasha spoke no English, we connected. As my church group prepared to depart, Sasha sat beside me, pulled a silver ring from his finger, and held it out for me to take. My eyes filled with tears and I spoke the only Russian word I knew—"Nyet, nyet." (No, no.) This child, who had nothing in the world to call his own except this ring, desperately wanted to give this ring to me. When asked why he wanted to give his only possession away, Sasha responded through an interpreter, "Because I am so thankful Scott came." For Sasha, abundant joy, extreme poverty, and a heart filled with gratitude overflowed in a wealth of generosity.

For many of us who have so much, we want more. We are not thankful for what we have and always look for the "something more." And truth be told, it's never enough. What would happen if, by God's grace, our desire to gain more and have more could be transformed by gratitude into a heartfelt desire to give more? What would happen if in a spirit of gratitude, we spent as much time figuring out ways to give as we spend figuring out how to earn, have, and keep?

Your Gratitude Story

- Can you recall a time when you were truly thankful in spite of negative circumstances?
- What are you most deeply grateful for?
- Can you recall a time when someone who could least afford it gave you a generous gift? What was it like? How did you respond? Did it affect you in any way?
- Can you recall a time when you were particularly generous? What was it like? What did you learn? How has it impacted your life?
- Does what I give in money, time, talent, and service reflect the depth of my gratitude?

Prayer of Gratitude

Oh God, thank you for the examples of gratitude and generosity you have sent into our lives. Forgive us, Lord, for being more concerned with how much we can earn, have, and keep, instead of being thankful for all we have. Forgive me for worrying about what I have or don't have. Help me, God, to be truly grateful and abundantly generous. Amen

Gather the recruits back together and have them discuss in groups of two or three their response to the questions. Then invite the entire group to join in discussion and reflection.

Additional Scripture on Gratitude

Psalm 107:1 CEB
Give thanks to the LORD because he is good, because his faithful love lasts forever!

Ephesians 1:15-16 CEB
Since I heard about your faith in the Lord Jesus and your love for all God's people, this is the reason that I don't stop giving thanks to God for you when I remember you in my prayers.

Ephesians 5:20 CEB
Always give thanks to God the Father for everything in the name of our Lord Jesus Christ.

Colossians 3:15-17 CEB
The peace of Christ must control your hearts—a peace into which you were called in one body. And be thankful people. The word of Christ must live in you richly. Teach and warn each other with all wisdom by singing psalms, hymns, and spiritual songs. Sing to God with gratitude in your hearts. Whatever you do, whether in speech or action, do it all in the name of the Lord Jesus and give thanks to God the Father through him.

1 Thessalonians 5:18 CEB
Give thanks in every situation because this is God's will for you in Christ Jesus.

James 1:17 CEB
Every good gift, every perfect gift, comes from above. These gifts come down from the Father, the creator of the heavenly lights, in whose character there is no change at all.

Prayerful Willingness

Remember, stewardship is grounded in gratitude, revealed in prayer, and lived in faith. The second core value of the revolution is prayer. When I acknowledge God as the source of everything I have, the question becomes, *What does God want to do with me and everything God has given me?* Gratitude combined with prayer is radical and life changing. Gratitude and prayer completely reorients our lives from self-centered to God-centered and kingdom-centered. Nouwen says this about prayer: "Prayer is the radical starting point of fund-raising because in prayer we slowly experience a reorientation of all our thoughts and feelings about ourselves and others."[6]

6. Nouwen, *The Spirituality of Fundraising*, 34.

Radical reorientation occurs as we cultivate what I refer to as a prayerful attitude of willingness. Prayerful willingness is, in its simplest form, a willingness to be open to the desires and will of God. Prayerful willingness is exemplified in the Horizons Stewardship capital campaign prayer, *Lord, what do you want to do through me?* When Yahweh appeared to Moses and called him to confront Pharaoh, eventually Moses was prayerfully willing and the world was forever changed. When God called Abram to leave his home, Abram was prayerfully willing, he went, and again the world was changed. In the garden, Jesus made it clear he did not want to suffer and die, but in the end, he was prayerfully willing and the world was forever changed.

Jim's Prayerful Willingness Story

Jim epitomizes the American success story. Jim didn't graduate from college but went to work immediately after high school. Eventually, Jim started his own business and through incredible hard work, a little bit of luck, and lots of prayer, Jim's business took off and succeeded beyond his wildest dreams. Jim has a beautiful home and a loving family. Jim attends church and even gives and by all appearances, gives generously. For Jim, everything changed when he prayed the prayer, *Lord, what do you want to do through me?* Jim experienced what Nouwen calls a "radical reorientation." Prayer completely changed his perspective on his work and business, on giving, and in fact on all of life. Jim went from working for himself and his family to working for God and the kingdom. After the devastating earthquake in Haiti, Jim traveled to Haiti as part of a medical mission team. Jim now spends two weeks of every year on mission trips. He sponsors youth so they can be a part of mission trips. Now, Jim's priority is not retirement at fifty-five to play golf and travel but retirement at fifty-five to spend more time and energy on mission work. Jim likes to tell people, "I'm not living the American dream; I'm living God's dream." Now that is radical reorientation. That is a revolution in generosity.

Find and invite someone like Jim in your congregation or in the community to share his or her story with your boot camp recruits. Invite your recruits to go off by themselves and reflect on the story they just heard and the following devotion.

> But we have this treasure in clay pots so that the awesome power belongs to God and doesn't come from us. (2 Cor 4:7 CEB)

You see, my friends, it's not about being right, not about being perfect. And most assuredly it is not always about doing the right thing. Noah, Abraham, and Moses all made mistakes, sometimes real whoppers! But in the end each was prayerfully willing. In their willingness God did something incredible and miraculous. Miracles occur when ordinary people like you and me prayerfully and willingly place ourselves in the hands of an extraordinary God. Let's read that sentence again:

> Miracles occur when ordinary people like you and me prayerfully and willingly place ourselves in the hands of an extraordinary God.

A cashier in a school cafeteria makes it her ministry to let each child know he or she is loved and special. A young girl working at Starbucks commits herself to being a blessing to each person she serves. A young boy tells his mother he is giving everything in his piggy bank to his church's building campaign. When asked why, he replies, "Because I want other kids to come and meet Jesus." The world changes when ordinary people willingly and prayerfully place themselves in the hands of an extraordinary God.

So what keeps you from fully saying yes to God: too weak, too sinful, too ordinary? Join the club! Join the club of ordinary people placing themselves in the hands of an extraordinary God.

Your Prayerful Willingness Story

- Can you describe a time when prayer changed you?
- Is there anything that holds you back from fully saying yes to God? If so, what?
- Can you recall a time when you were prayerfully willing? Have you ever prayed something like, *God what do you want to do through me?* What happened?
- What might it mean for you to pray, God, what do you want to do with my money, my possessions, and my life?

Dear God, help me today in this moment to willingly place my hands in yours. Help me today to prayerfully and willingly love and serve you and those you bring into my presence. God, what do you want to do through me? Amen.

Gather the recruits back together and have them discuss in groups of two or three their response to the questions. Then invite the entire group to join in discussion and reflection.

Scriptures on Prayerful Willingness
Genesis 6–7, The story of Noah

Genesis 12, The story of Abram

Exodus 3, The story of Moses

Luke 1:38 CEB
Then Mary said, "I am the Lord's servant. Let it be with me just as you have said."

Matthew 4:18-20 CEB
As Jesus walked alongside the Galilee Sea, he saw two brothers, Simon, who is called Peter, and Andrew, throwing fishing nets into the sea, because they were fishermen. "Come, follow me," he said, "and I'll show you how to fish for people." Right away, they left their nets and followed him.

Luke 22:41-44 CEB
He withdrew from them about a stone's throw, knelt down, and prayed. He said, "Father, if it's your will, take this cup of suffering away from me. However, not my will but your will must be done." Then a heavenly angel appeared to him and strengthened him. He was in anguish and prayed even more earnestly. His sweat became like drops of blood falling on the ground.

Faith—A Bold Step

The core values of a generosity revolution are gratitude, prayer, and faith. Gratitude and prayer will, on their own, bring about what Nouwen refers to as a radical reorientation to life. The very ground of my existence changes when I realize that all I have comes from God and not the work of my own hands. All of a sudden my core identity shifts when I acknowledge God as the source and the giver of life—all that I have and all that I am. Gratitude and prayer subvert the basic message of our culture: my job, my bank account, the car I drive, the home I live in—these things determine who I am. Gratitude and prayer scream loudly, "I am not a product of what I own or the money I make; I am a child of God, created in the image of God." Remember our big picture:

> We hold these truths to be self-evident that all people are created in the image of a loving, giving, and generous God. We believe real life, true liberty, and eternal joy are only realized when we live lives of abundant generosity and sacrificial love.

Gratitude and prayer subvert the message of our culture, but true revolution occurs only as we embrace the third core value of our revolution—faith. Faith puts legs on gratitude and prayer; faith moves the revolution from the pew to the battlefield. In faith, we act out what we believe in gratitude and prayer. In essence, faith answers the question, so what and what's next? Faith is gratitude and prayer in action.

Faith, when understood as what's next or now what, calls people to step out of their comfort zone and embrace the call of God revealed in prayerful willingness. Faith could be the simple filling out of a pledge card for the first time. Faith could be making a commitment to tithe after a lifetime of token giving. Faith could be attending a Bible study or going on a mission trip for the first time.

Two Contrasting Faith Stories

As we think about the importance of faith in our generosity revolution, let's return to two characters from earlier devotions. The rich young man, as found in Mark 10 and written about in chapter 1, clearly describes a good young man, a man who obeys the rules and laws of his religion. Gratitude and prayer are undoubtedly part of his life. In prayerful willingness the young man approaches Jesus and asks a form of our question, "Lord, what do you want to do through me?" When Jesus responds with the answer, "Sell all you have and give it to the poor," this young man opts out of the revolution. For whatever reason, he can't step out of his comfort zone. He cannot make the step of faith. For our rich young man, the revolution ends before it really started.

Compare the story of our rich young man with the story of Miss Charlotte as told in chapter 2. If you recall, Miss Charlotte fully embraced both the attitude of gratitude and a willingness to ask God, *What would you have me do?* In the midst of bankruptcy, driven by gratitude and prayer, Miss Charlotte petitioned the court to allow her to continue her tithe to her church. Then in another incredible act of faith Miss Charlotte said, "I will make a pledge to the capital campaign as soon as I emerge from bankruptcy. I am not sure how, but I know I will pledge and give something." Let the revolution begin! Gratitude, prayer, and faith.

Ask your boot camp recruits if they have ever stepped out in faith and what the results were. You might also ask if there has ever been a time when they knew they were being called to step out in faith and, like the rich young man, said no. Ask them to discuss what prevents us from stepping out in faith. Invite your recruits to go off by themselves and reflect on what they have heard and the following devotion: "Faith is the reality of what we hope for, the proof of what we don't see. The elders in the past were approved because they showed faith. By faith we understand that the universe has been created by a word from God so that the visible came into existence from the invisible" (Heb 11:1-3 CEB).

Julie's life has not been easy. She was raised in scarcity and would steal change from her mother's pocketbook just to get something to eat. Then at the age of twelve her only daughter was stricken with leukemia and not expected to live. Julie herself has endured numerous surgeries just to be able to function and get around. Now her church is having a capital campaign and she was asked to give. Her first response was, "No way." All of those early childhood memories of scarcity reared their ugly head. But as Julie spoke last night she said, "Something strange began to happen as I asked myself, what do I have to be grateful for?" In spite of all her struggles Julie began to realize how God had blessed her and all the many reasons she had to be grateful. Gratitude moved Julie from scarcity to abundance and fear to faith. She made the single largest gift of her life. And she said to the group, "I don't know where it's coming from; this is truly a gift given in faith and I am counting on the assurance of things not seen."

Each day we are all faced with a choice. We can chose to either live in scarcity and fear or we can choose to live in abundance and faith with *the assurance of things hoped for, the conviction of things not seen.*

Your Faith Story

- Can you recall a time when you knew God was calling you to step out in faith and because of fear you said no? What happened?
- Can you recall a time when God called you to step out in faith and you said yes, in spite of fear? What happened?
- Are there memories of scarcity or lack that might prevent you from truly giving in faith?

Dear God, it is so very easy for me to see all of the things wrong in my life, all the things I don't have. Forgive me for focusing on scarcity and fear. Give me the courage, oh God, to live a life of abundance and faith. Amen.

Scripture for Faith—A Bold Step

Matthew 17:20, The Faith of a Mustard Seed

Matthew 14:28-31, Peter Walking on Water

Mark 2:1-12, Healing of the Paralytic

1 Corinthians 2:3-5 CEB
I stood in front of you with weakness, fear, and a lot of shaking. My message and my preaching weren't presented with convincing wise words but with a demonstration of the Spirit and of power. I did this so that your faith might not depend on the wisdom of people but on the power of God.

2 Corinthians 5:6-7 CEB
So we are always confident, because we know that while we are living in the body, we are away from our home with the Lord. We live by faith and not by sight.

Generosity Declaration

After discussion, inform the recruits that now the time has come to craft your group's Generosity Declaration. A Generosity Declaration has three basic parts:

- This is what I believe.
- This is what I will do.
- This is what I challenge others to do.

Some questions to consider:

- What do I believe about God and my identity as a child of God?
- What money baggage have I been carrying, and how has it impacted my relationship with money, giving, and God?
- What do I believe about the source of joy and meaning in life?
- What do I believe about gratitude and prayer?
- What do I believe about my responsibility to give generously, to tithe?
- What do I believe about my need to be in service and mission?
- What is God calling me to do? How is God calling me to live?
- How am I going to live differently?

Invite your recruits to break off by themselves and begin to answer the above questions. Then invite them to share their responses with two or three others and see if there are ways they can be combined into one statement. Then invite the small groups to share their results with the large group and discuss what should be included in the group's Generosity Declaration. You don't need to worry about coming up with a completely polished product. Just come up with the outline. You may choose to share a few examples.

Generosity Declaration Example #1

Here is an example of a Generosity Declaration adapted from the Standing Commission on Stewardship and Development, *Report to the 75th General Episcopal Convention.*

WE BELIEVE in a generous, loving, and self-giving God.

WE BELIEVE:

- All that we are and all that we have comes from God.
- God has been generous to us so that we can be generous to others.

37

- We are a society challenged by addictive, self-destructive relationships with money and possessions.
- Christ longs to set us free from this bondage and restore us to life-giving relationships with God, one another, and creation.

WE COMMIT OURSELVES TO:

- Staying close to Jesus, who is the one who revitalizes and transforms us.
- Discerning God's will for our lives through the holy habits of daily prayer, study, weekly worship, observing the Sabbath, tithing, and other intentional spiritual practices.
- Living enthusiastically, sharing ourselves (all that we are) and our gifts from God (all that we have) to be instruments of God's reconciling love in the world.
- Giving to God the first portion of our time, talent, money, and all our resources—not merely the leftovers.

WE PLEDGE OURSELVES to dare to imagine, initiate, and create personal and corporate ministries that can be outward and visible signs of God's kingdom on earth.

WE INVITE our church family to join us in this lifelong, joyful, transforming, and liberating response to God's call to us.

St. Paul's United Methodist Church in State College, Pennsylvania, has the following statement on their website.

We believe Stewardship is:

- a covenant relationship with God that begins in prayer and calls us to engage the gospel
- the call to follow the example of Christ to love one another and care for our neighbor
- the belief that we are called to give proportionally of our time, talent, and treasure, with tithing as the goal.

We, the Leadership of St. Paul's, with God's help, commit to:

- lead our congregation in fostering and strengthening our commitment to Christ

- actively participate in nurturing a proper understanding of stewardship throughout the congregation
- use our time and talents to uphold the church through our prayers, our presence, gifts, service, and witness
- give our treasures on a proportional basis toward, to and beyond the tithe

We encourage you to:

- deepen your relationship with God through prayer and engaging the gospel in study
- trust in the Holy Spirit to lead and guide you through your stretching and changing of growth in your commitment to Christ this year
- renew your vows to uphold the church through your prayers, presence, gifts, service, and witness
- use your gifts by participating in the ministries of St. Paul's Church at home and in the world
- give faithfully and proportionally of your time, talent, and treasure.

Each of these statements contains the three necessary parts of our Generosity Declaration:

- This is what I believe.
- This is what I will do.
- This is what I challenge you to do.

Your Generosity Declaration

This is what I believe:

This is what I will do:

This is what I challenge you to do:

39

Next Steps

After returning home from your generosity boot camp, finalize your group's Generosity Declaration. Choose a Sunday to present your declaration to the congregation. All of the Generosity recruits should stand in front of the congregation and have two or three of the recruits give their personal reflections on how their life has been/will be changed because of their Generosity Declaration. Do not immediately ask the members of the congregation to "sign on the dotted line" to join the revolution. *Remember, the average member of the congregation has not gone on the journey. If you make "the ask" now the response will be lukewarm and limited.*

Do you recall the image of the dancing man in the open field? You've recruited a few people to join you, but now you need more. Your next task is to encourage the congregation to get up and join the dance, leading to revolution. If we do not intentionally invite and inspire the congregation to join, then the entire generosity team will be lone nuts and the revolution will fail. Here is an outline of how to encourage, invite, and inspire your congregation to join the generosity revolution. The following outline is based around four Sundays: Gratitude, Prayer, Faith, and then Commitment and signing of the Generosity Declaration. As you begin, display the Generosity Declaration banner in a prominent location in the sanctuary.

Sunday 1: Gratitude

The worship theme is gratitude/thankfulness. Use one of the scriptures under gratitude or even use the gratitude devotion as the message outline. Have one of your generosity recruits give witness to the power of gratitude. The end result is the recognition that all we have is a gift from the loving hand of God. At the conclusion of the message instruct the ushers to pass out 4x6 multicolored index cards and invite the congregation to write what they are most deeply grateful for, how they have been blessed. After a brief period of silence invite them to bring the cards forward and place in a special basket. After the cards have been filled out and returned, pass out a 21-Day Devotional. A sample is found at the end of the book. This same devotional can be downloaded for free at my website. Have hard copies distributed to each family and also plan on e-mailing them on a daily basis to your members. Tell them at the end of the four weeks they will be asked to join the Generosity Revolution. During the following week have the gratitude cards all posted in a prominent location. Be sure you have included children and youth.

Sunday 2: Prayer

The theme for worship is prayer as willingness. Again, use one of the scripture verses or the devotional on prayer. Have one of the recruits give testimony about prayer and the power of praying: "Lord, what do you want to do through me?" The person giving witness should also remind and encourage people to continue using the devotional guide. At the conclusion of the message invite those present to visibly demonstrate a willingness to commit to prayerful willingness. You might choose to pass out a magnet or some kind of reminder with the prayer printed on it, "Lord, what do you want to do through me?"

Sunday 3: Faith

The theme for worship centers on God's call to step out boldly in faith. Use the devotion on faith or choose one of the scriptures for the message. Have two people give witness to the power of stepping out boldly in faith. One of the people speaking should focus on stepping out in faith financially to tithe. Another should give witness on stepping out in faith to go on a mission trip or stretch in some way other than finances. At the conclusion of the service, pass out copies of the Generosity Declaration and let people know they will be asked to sign these during worship the following week.

Sunday 4: Commitment

The theme for this final Sunday will be encouraging people to come forward and sign the Generosity Declaration. During the message give opportunity for members of your team to talk about what the Generosity Declaration means for them personally. You might have three or four up front with you and conduct an informal interview/discussion. You might ask such questions as

- What has been the biggest change in your life since being part of the Generosity Revolution?
- What phrase in the Declaration means the most to you?
- What does being generous mean to you now?
- What was the hardest part about joining the revolution?

You might consider showing the video of the dancing man and then inviting the people to come and join the dance/revolution by signing the Generosity Declaration banner. Encourage the members of your team to lead the way in coming forward, even though they have already signed the banner.

In the weeks following the service make follow-up visits to the people who signed the banner. Listen, be encouraging, and help them find a way to concretely be a part of Generosity Rising and a true revolution in giving.

Chapter Four

Fan the Flame of Revolution

Because of this, I'm reminding you to revive God's gift that is in you through the laying on of my hands. God didn't give us a spirit that is timid but one that is powerful, loving, and self-controlled.

2 Tim 1:6-7 CEB

Congratulations. If you have followed the suggestions in chapters 1–3 then your revolution in generosity is underway. Are people complaining and murmuring yet? Have you heard any of these phrases?

- All this church cares about is my money.
- These are hard times and people are giving all they can.
- All this preacher talks about is money.
- You should mind your own business. Giving is between God and me.

Perhaps these comments, this opposition, and the criticism surprised you. Remember this sobering truth: not every uprising results in lasting revolution. Do you remember Tiananmen Square? In April 1989, hundreds of thousands of prodemocracy demonstrators descended on Tiananmen Square. Demonstrations quickly spread to other cities across China. Across the world, people wondered if they were watching the birth of a revolution. By the beginning of June, the government violently extinguished the flame of uprising and revolution.

Make no mistake, entrenched leaders with no desire or heart for generosity will fight to extinguish the revolution in generosity. Remember our named enemy: People love stuff and money more than God. People prefer building their own kingdom, which offers immediate gratification, rather than the kingdom of God, which can seem distant and intangible. People will fight to protect the "stuff" they love. Communist rulers in China were determined to protect their rule and power at all cost. The same will be true in your church. Those who love their "stuff" more than they love Jesus will attempt to extinguish the flame of your generosity revolution.

Pastor Susan's Story

After attending one of my Bounty Workshops Pastor Susan and her stewardship chair were determined to start their revolution in generosity. The two of them began discussing candidates for their team and were even beginning to plan their version of a Generosity Boot Camp. The small first flame of revolution was beginning to burn. Imagine their surprise when the treasurer and the chairperson of the leadership team introduced a motion to expressly forbid anyone other than the treasurer to have access to the giving records of the church. After all, they piously proclaimed, "giving is only between the giver and God." After serious discussion, the motion passed. Do not be surprised when opposition emerges to your revolution in generosity.

Your Story

Have you experienced opposition to your revolution? How/What?

Fanning the Flames

How do we fan the flame of an uprising in generosity until the flame becomes the burning fire of a lasting revolution?

Please remember the image of the shirtless dancing man. If you try and do this by yourself you will simply be the lone nut dancing in the middle of the field. Lone nuts are easy to dismiss. Lone nuts become easily discouraged and will quit dancing. Do not underestimate the importance of chapter 1. You must begin to surround yourself with other believers in the cause of generosity. As opposition mounts, and it will, we need to remember the sacred task before us. Remember our place of surpassing importance.

> We hold these truths to be self-evident that all people are created in the image of a loving, giving, and generous God. We believe real life, true liberty, and eternal joy are only realized when we live lives of abundant generosity and sacrificial love.

Remember, what we are doing is nothing short of enabling individuals to become the very people God created them to be. Remember, we are inviting people on a novel journey of surpassing importance. *This is a sacred journey.* It is a journey of becoming the person God created from the beginning of all creation.

Examine Your Church's Current Practices

With your team in place, the place of surpassing importance squarely in front of you, the Generosity Declaration signed and displayed; your next step will be to evaluate your church's current practices regarding giving and generosity. There are six general areas you will evaluate. At the end of the book these six categories are put into the format of a Generosity Survey.

A Clear and Compelling Vision

In *Climb Higher: Reaching New Heights in Giving and Generosity*, I lift up the fundamental importance of a clear and compelling vision for mission and ministry. If you want your revolution in generosity to be more than a temporary uprising, you need to be able to answer the question "Why?" Why should people give their hard-earned dollars to your church? Because "we are the church" is no longer a sufficient answer. Clif Christopher, in his book *Not Your Parent's Offering Plate*, lists the five reasons people give. The number one reason people give to any institution is a belief in the mission of the organization.[1] I give to the American Cancer Society because I believe they save lives by finding cures for cancer. I give to the Salvation Army because I believe in what they do when tragedy or disaster strikes anywhere in the world. I give to dig wells in Malawi because I know the difference clean water makes for an entire village.

Do you remember Steve from the introduction? As we shared breakfast, Steve was seriously questioning his giving to the church. Steve gives over and above a tithe but is considering cutting back on his giving to the church—not his overall giving, just his giving to the church. Let me share with you Steve's comments again: "I don't see lives being changed. The other organizations are changing lives; why shouldn't I just give it all to them?" In Christianity Today's *Leadership Journal*, I found an interesting article

---

1. Clif Christopher, *Not Your Parent's Offering Plate* (Nashville: Abingdon Press, 2008), 12.

entitled "Why I Won't Give to Your Church." Robert Jewe begins his open letter to churches with the following line: "I am a 23-year-old who refuses to give to your church." He then continues,

> Where exactly is our money going? Is it helping others? Or is it being spent on elaborate Christmas pageants? Are you building the kingdom? Or are you building your kingdom?...What are you doing in your community? Are you feeding and clothing the homeless? Are you hosting support groups for addicts? Are you finding childcare for single parents? These are things my generation respects. We want to help the people around us. You'll win us over if you do the same.[2]

Millennials, Baby Boomers, Gen Xers—the names or ages don't seem to matter; everyone wants to know their giving is being used to change people's lives. Chuck Lawless, currently professor of evangelism and missions and dean of graduate studies at Southeastern Seminary, in a blog entitled "10 Ways to Improve Giving in Your Church," writes,

> God's people are not opposed to giving; they are opposed to supporting a weak or unclear purpose. Churches that seek dollars simply to keep their doors open to minister to their own people aren't likely to garner support from a young generation committed to the nations. Ask your congregation to state your church's vision in a single sentence; if most can't do it, I suspect you're missing out on financial support as well.[3]

Suggestions to Develop a Clear and Compelling Vision

A compelling vision for ministry is not about paying the bills, paying the pastor, or keeping the doors open; a compelling vision for ministry focuses on changed lives. Please note, having a compelling vision for ministry does not equal having a vision statement. Many churches I have been in have a vision statement, but frankly, no vision for a ministry that changes people's lives. Conversely, some of the most exciting and growing churches I have been in have no formal vision statement but have a clear and compelling vision for how God is changing lives in their particular community. Here are a few simple questions to ask yourself.

---

2. Robert Jewe, "Why I Won't Give to Your Church," *Leadership Journal*, spring 2013, www.christianitytoday.com/le/2013/spring/why-i-wont-give-to-your -church.html.

3. Thom S. Rainer, "10 Ideas to Improve Giving in Your Church," April 29, 2014, http://thomrainer.com/2014/04/29/10-ideas-improve-giving-church/.

- Why do I attend my church or why do I give money to my church?
- What makes my church different from all the other churches in our community?
- What is the one thing we are passionate about as a church?

The answers you give will begin to shed light on your church's vision for ministry and mission. Is this vision compelling? Does this vision make a difference in people's lives, in our community, or in the world? Is the vision about changed lives?

Another great way to find out your church's real vision for mission and ministry is to attend a leadership meeting and watch what happens when a new idea for a program or ministry is proposed. If the discussion focuses on how much a program or ministry costs, then there is no real compelling vision for mission and ministry. The only question that really counts when someone proposes something new is, Will this move our vision for mission and ministry forward? If the answer to this question is no then it doesn't matter how worthy the idea is. If the answer to this question is yes, and God is calling you to this ministry, then it doesn't matter how much it costs.

You can also begin to understand your real vision for mission and ministry by asking people in the community, "What is our church known for?" Pay attention to the answer because the answer will give you insight into your real vision, not your stated vision. You might also ask someone not familiar with your congregation to look at your website, read your newsletter and bulletins, and even attend worship. Then ask them, "What do you think we are passionate about? What do you think drives us as a congregation?" This exercise requires courage because the answers will be revealing and usually surprising. When I read newsletters and bulletins I often think the church's vision for ministry is to hold the world's largest yard sale, wash the most cars, or sell the most cookies.

Make no mistake, if your church does not have a clear and compelling vision for ministry, mission, and changed lives, your revolution in generosity will fail. Conversely, a clear and compelling vision for ministry will indeed fan the flame of revolution, helping ensure your revolution will be more than just a temporary uprising.

What do you do if your church struggles with a clear and compelling vision for mission and ministry? You might consider this two-step process first outlined in *Bounty*.

1. Set up individual interviews with your top twenty givers and ask some of the following questions:

   • What do you love most about your church? What ministry are you passionate about in your church?
   • What sets you apart from other churches?
   • If you had a million-dollar gift given to the church, where would you spend it?
   • What do you believe are the greatest ministry needs within your community?

2. After talking with some of your leaders and top givers, conduct a series of home gatherings and ask the same questions listed above.

If in the interview process you uncover some leaders/givers that are clearly excited and enthusiastic about the church's mission and ministry, invite them to be host families for these gatherings. At these gatherings you should also be prepared to present demographic information about your community. MissionInsite and Percept are a few places you can purchase demographic information. Check with your denomination because many denominations provide such information free. Also consider speaking with school principals, superintendents, local politicians, chief of police, and other community leaders to learn more about the needs of your particular community.

Another possibility for a church without vision is to hire a consulting firm to assist you in the process. Auxano, a group founded by the author of *Church Unique*, Will Mancini, is one such firm. Horizons Stewardship and many other firms also assist churches in vision and mission.

Resources to Help Develop a Clear and Compelling Vision

Barna, George. *The Power of Vision: Discover and Apply God's Plan for Your Life and Ministry.* Baker Book House, 2009.

Drucker, Peter, et al. *The Five Most Important Questions You Will Ever Ask about Your Organization.* San Francisco: Jossey-Bass, 2008.

Mancini, Will. *Church Unique: How Missional Leaders Cast Vision, Capture Culture, and Create Movement.* Leadership Network Series. San Francisco: Jossey-Bass, 2008.

McNeal, Reggie. *Missional Renaissance: Changing the Scorecard for the Church.* Leadership Network Series. San Francisco: Jossey-Bass, 2009.

Tell Stories of Changed Lives

A revolutionary vision for a compelling ministry that changes and transforms lives does no good when no one hears the story. Remember the breakfast conversation with my friend Steve? Steve questioned giving his tithe to the church because he did not see lives being changed. I would wager that many lives had been changed in that little church but no one told the story. Look again at the open letter from the millennial who does not give to the church:

> Where exactly is our money going? Is it helping others? Or is it being spent on elaborate Christmas pageants? Are you building the kingdom? Or are you building your kingdom?... What are you doing in your community? Are you feeding and clothing the homeless? Are you hosting support groups for addicts? Are you finding childcare for single parents? These are things my generation respects. We want to help the people around us. You'll win us over if you do the same.

Perhaps the key sentence in the letter is the second sentence: *Is it helping others?* Most of the churches I have been in do in fact help others, and yes, lives are being changed, but again, *no one tells the story.* During a presentation on vision at a local church a participant said, "Here is our newsletter. It is well written, in fact, beautifully put together but we tell no story of change or transformation. We talk about the upcoming sermon series and our upcoming events but nothing about how our church changes lives."

One of my all-time favorite stories is the story of the golden Buddha of Bangkok. I tell the story in *Climb Higher* and retell it here for a very different purpose. When the Burmese were about to attack Bangkok, the monks took their prized possession, a solid-gold Buddha, and covered the priceless statue in mud and plaster. Tragically, all of the monks were killed and there was no one left to tell the story. This priceless golden statue became a statue of mud and plaster because no one could tell the story. How many of our churches have covered their priceless stories of changed lives with mud and plaster until finally the golden statue is nothing but clay? All because we fail to tell the story! And when we fail to tell our story, people like Steve and the young millennial stop giving. Every newsletter, every worship service, every bulletin, every Facebook post, and every tweet: all are opportunities to tell stories of change and transformation. And as an aside, if you really can't come up with any stories of change and transformation, put a For Sale sign in front of your church.

Suggestions for Telling Your Story

If, like most churches, you are not effectively telling your story, here are some practical suggestions.

1. Every staff meeting and every leadership meeting should have time on the agenda for sharing stories of change and transformation. One of my finance chairs now deliberately begins every meeting with stories of ministry, change, and transformation instead of looking at the balance sheet. He will tell you, people actually look forward to their meetings! Can you imagine a finance meeting in which people actually look forward to attending? One senior pastor said the sharing of stories completely changed staff morale and brought staff together in ways never before seen.

   - Do we?_____
     Can we?_____

2. Look at every communication piece your church has produced over the last six months and ask the question, how often are we telling stories? How can we use our newsletter, our worship services, our webpage, our Facebook page, our Twitter account to tell stories?

   - Do we?_____
     Can we?_____

3. Use video clips and other creative ideas to give people opportunities during worship to tell the story of how God changed their lives. A development office for a university told me he would die to have a chance to bring all of his donors together once a week and hear students and former students tell their stories. We have the opportunity. Why don't we use it?

   - Do we?_____
     Can we?_____

4. At least once a year have a major celebration of ministry and changed lives. Consider something like Cardboard Testimonies. If you have never heard of Cardboard Testimonies, Google it. In *Bounty*, chapter 7, there is an extensive discussion of how to effectively use Cardboard Testimonies and tips for implementing it in your church. You can also find examples of Cardboard Testimonies on my website.

- Do we?_____
  Can we?_____

During a recent capital campaign a potential major donor made it very clear that she was not going to participate in any meaningful way. She would not attend any of the campaign meetings and she would not pledge. But then her church used Cardboard Testimonies during the campaign. When the service was over she shook the pastor's hand and said, "That was the most meaningful service I have ever witnessed. You need to show the video of those testimonies tonight at the campaign meeting and I will be there." Of course we showed the video, she was present, and a significant gift was made. The mud and plaster had been chipped away and the glorious, priceless, golden statue of change and transformation was there for all to see. Tell your story, tell God's story, and the flickering flame of revolution will burn bright.

Make It Easy and Convenient for People to Give

With over 150 people in the room, my colleague and founder of Horizons, Clif Christopher, asked the question, "How many people here pay for their gas at the pump with a credit or debit card?" Nearly everyone in the room raised their hand. He then asked, "How many of you regularly walk inside and give the attendant cash?" Maybe two people raised their hand. Typically, when I pull into a gas station that does not have a pay-at-the-pump feature, I go someplace else. The same dynamic happens to me in nearly every church I attend. As a consultant I travel all over this great country of ours. And I usually do it with zero cash in my wallet. So what happens when I attend one of my churches? We get to the point in the worship service where the offering is about to be taken. I become nervous and start to sweat. I fearfully open my wallet hoping and praying I will find at least a dollar bill.

Usually it's empty, and I sheepishly pass the plate without putting anything in. How many times have you gone to church and a special offering was taken for a tragedy or natural disaster and you had little or nothing to give? What would have happened if you had the chance to give via a QR code or, God forbid, a giving kiosk that accepts credit and debit cards?

On the other hand, one of my churches sent out an e-mail telling multiple stories of how their ministries were impacting the local community. I was truly impressed. Then as I got to the end of the e-mail there was a request for money. Immediately following the request was a big green button that said "Give." I had just received some unexpected money from a workshop and on the spur of the moment, I hit the big green "Give" button. Within a few minutes I made a fairly significant gift.

Do you remember when the Internet was becoming popular? People were wondering, *What good is this? Why would we need to have the Internet in our church?* Now, almost every church I go to not only has Internet but Wi-Fi as well. The same thing is going to happen with electronic giving, credit card giving, QR codes, and giving kiosks. Every church will eventually have them. The only question is whether you will be on the leading edge or frantically trying to play catch-up somewhere down the road. Giving needs to be easy and convenient. There is nothing particularly holy or righteous about making people give only cash or checks, and only in the offering plate on Sunday morning.

Even with a clear and compelling vision, even when we tell stories of changed lives, we need to make sure people are given multiple opportunities to give in a variety of easy and convenient ways. Guess what? If you choose to *not* make giving easy and convenient, your local university will be happy to step in and take your place.

What if you are one of those churches that only takes cash or checks, and only on Sunday mornings? Here are some ways to fan the flame of revolution by making giving easy and convenient.

Suggestions for Making Giving Easy and Convenient

1. When sending out e-mails and other forms of electronic communication, always include a "Give" button or link. Test the link or button and make sure it is indeed both easy and convenient. I used a QR code in a church to support a particular mission and it was so difficult I almost gave up.

- Do we?_____
  Can we?_____

2. Make sure on your home page there is a clearly visible "Donate" or "Give" button. Again, make sure it is both easy and convenient to use.

- Do we?_____
  Can we?_____

3. Look into using QR codes, giving kiosks, square readers, and even text giving. If you have no idea what I'm talking about, ask a millennial.

- Do we?_____
  Can we?_____

4. As soon as you receive a gift make sure an appropriate acknowledgment and thank-you is sent. Here is a word of warning: some of these are automatically generated and you need to check the wording to make sure it is appropriate for a church and not just any business. I received an automated thank-you from one electronic gift and it said, "Thank you for your transaction, we've enjoyed doing business with you." Not good!

- Do we?_____
  Can we?_____

Say Thank You

Most of us were taught as children to always say thank you. Somehow the church seems to have forgotten this early childhood lesson. When I am leading my workshop called "Unlocking the Secrets of Bountiful

Generosity," I always ask the participants to raise their hands if they have made a gift to a charity other than the church in the last six months. Usually nearly everyone raises their hand. Then I ask, how many received a thank-you? Again, nearly everyone raises their hand. Then I ask how many have given to their church in the last six months. Everyone raises their hand. You know where I'm going. I then ask how many have received a thank-you. Very few people, in very few workshops, ever raise their hand.

Dr. Robert Emmons, professor of psychology at the University of California in Davis and a researcher in the psychology of gratitude, says "gratitude serves as a key link in the dynamic between receiving and giving. It is not only a response to kindnesses received, but it is also a motivator of future benevolent actions on the part of the recipient."[4]

Evidently universities have gotten the message that expressing gratitude is not only the right and polite thing to do but also leads to increased generosity. In a quick Google search I found webpages for both Rutgers University and Duke University that instruct students on the importance of expressing thanks to donors who fund their scholarships. The Department of Donor Relations at Rutgers University has a webpage called "Thank You 101: A Guide to Expressing Appreciation for Your Scholarship." The first section in their guide is called "Why Should I Say THANKS?"

> Rutgers University alumni and friends make contributions to scholarship funds that help pay for your education. You already know that when you receive a gift, saying thank you is the right thing to do. The scholarship you received is a gift; a note of thanks to the donor is a great way to express your appreciation.

> Nothing is more welcome than a thoughtful note of thanks. A well-written thank you reflects favorably on you and is important to the scholarship donors. They look forward to getting to know who they are helping by learning about your interests and goals. A short note from you affirms the value and significance of their contributions and encourages their continued support.[5]

Look at the last sentence again: "A short note from you affirms the value and significance of their contributions and encourages their continued support." We in the church have been hesitant to do this for fear that we might offend the person who does not give. We must reverse this think-

---

4. "Is Gratitude the Queen of the Virtues?" Big Questions, last modified September 18, 2012, www.bigquestionsonline.com/content/gratitude-queen-virtues.
5. https://studentaid.rutgers.edu/forms/thankyou.pdf.

ing. A small urban church read my book *Bounty* and decided to take the risk and intentionally went to their top ten givers for the sole purpose of saying thank you. Two laypeople, not the pastor, made phone calls and actually went to visit these top ten givers for the sole purpose of saying thank you. No, they didn't know the individual amounts, just that they were in the top ten. I later met with the two individuals who made the visits, and they related how incredibly enriching and spiritually powerful the visits were for them. No one was offended or put off. No one was irate and said, "How do you know I give?" Instead the visits focused on the love the givers had for their church and why their church was so important to them. Why do they give so generously? The visitors described being humbled and incredibly blessed by these conversations. They didn't ask for an increase in giving or anything else. They simply said thank you and then listened.

Guidelines for Saying Thank You

In a wonderful blog entitled "Why Thanking Donors Online Is Powerful," Simon Norris and Juliet Richardson give guidelines for saying thank you that will be helpful for your church and in particular your Generosity Committee. Below are a few of their suggestions.[6]

1. *Say thank you.* Make sure your people understand you are saying thank you for a gift and not simply giving them a receipt for a business transaction. Make sure this is true for online giving and regular plate giving. Those wonderful quarterly or yearly statements should be personalized and should in fact be more thank oriented than statement or receipt oriented.

   - Do we?_____
     Can we?_____

2. *Make it personal.* Use people's names when you send a thank-you. Names make us feel special and important. Don't you just love the letter from your church that starts with "Dear Friend of…"? Does it take more time and effort to add personal names? Yes! But it is time and effort well spent. Here is what Simon and Juliet say about this:

---

6. www.nomensa.com/blog/2012/why-thanking-donors-online-is-powerful.

Putting the donor's name into a thank you message will make it stand out and feel special. So, make the thank you message as personal as possible: include the donor's name and the amount they have given (for example, "Thank you Simon for your generous donation of £25…"). This acts as confirmation of the donation that they have made, as well as helping to reinforce positive feelings and make them feel personally thanked.

- Do we?_____
  Can we?_____

3. *Show them the difference their donation will make.* Remember people give because they want to make a difference in other people's lives. Every statement and every thank-you should include a ministry story of how your church is making a difference. Again, use video and pictures to tell a story of ministry and transformation. Showing the donor that their donation has been worthwhile is very important and is something that comes up every time we do usability testing on donation journeys. Showing them the difference that their donations will make and how the money will be used will make donors feel that it was worthwhile to give.[7]

- Do we?_____
  Can we?_____

4. *Do not ask for additional financial support.* How many times have you gotten a thank-you from your church and in the end the thank-you was just another way to ask for more money? The plea for more money in a thank-you note negates all of the positive reinforcement accomplished by the thank-you.

- Do we?_____
  Can we?_____

7. Ibid.

Suggestions for Saying Thank You

If saying thank you is a growing edge for your church in fanning the flame of generosity, then here are a few suggestions.

1. Make use of two- to three-minute videos in worship of people saying thank you. Encourage people who have been blessed and touched by a particular ministry to say thank you.

   - Do we?_____
     Can we?_____

2. Have a gratitude wall in your church and encourage people to put notes on it. Have a gratitude page on your website and have it highly visible, not hidden away. Encourage your people to go online to post a gratitude note. Be real bold and at the end of a message on gratitude ask people to pull out their smartphones and post something online during worship. For those without a smartphone or tablet, have index cards available.

   - Do we?_____
     Can we?_____

3. After any significant event in your church consider having a thank-a-thon. Have your leaders come to the church with cell phones and make calls to all of the volunteers that made your event possible. Can you imagine the positive reactions you would get if you called all of your VBS volunteers for the sole reason of saying thank you?

   - Do we?_____
     Can we?_____

4. Turn your financial statements into thank-you notes and include a story of ministry.

   - Do we?_____
     Can we?_____

5. Make saying thank you a significant focal point of the Generosity Committee. One church even changed the name of the Stewardship Committee to the Gratitude Team.

   - Do we?_____
     Can we?_____

6. Consider having special dinners or desserts for your givers with the expressed purpose of saying thank you and demonstrating where their money has been used over the last twelve months. Conclude these meetings with a description of ministry you hope to accomplish in the next twelve months. You *do not* ask for money at this time. These meetings are for saying thank you and casting vision. Michael Slaughter at Ginghamsburg United Methodist Church recommends what he refers to as Kingdom Investor meetings. In the fall he holds two such meetings: one for those who give $10,000 and above, and a separate one for those who give $1,000-$9,999. Michael gives a thorough description of these, complete with agendas, invitations, and phone scripts in his book *Money Matters: Financial Freedom for all God's Churches.*[8]

   - Do we?_____
     Can we?_____

Saying thank you in a variety of ways and in multiple settings will indeed fan the flame of generosity and help keep your revolution burning bright.

Set High Expectations

Your generosity revolution is underway and momentum is clearly building. Excitement grows as you articulate a vision for ministry clearly focused on changing lives. And then you hit a wall. Oftentimes the wall takes the form of entrenched leadership unwilling to change, unwilling to join you in this glorious revolution of generosity. Let me remind you of what I said in the opening of this chapter:

8. Michael Slaughter with Kim Miller, *Money Matters: Financial Freedom for all God's Churches* (Nashville: Abingdon Press, 2006).

Make no mistake, entrenched leaders with no desire or heart for generosity will fight to extinguish the revolution in generosity. Remember our named enemy: People love stuff and money more than God. People prefer building their own kingdom, which offers immediate gratification, rather than the kingdom of God, which can seem distant and intangible. People will fight to protect the "stuff" they love.

This may be the number one threat to the survival of and continued growth of your revolution in generosity. How do we deal with entrenched leadership who threaten to extinguish this spreading flame of generosity? Let me share an example.

The capital campaign had been incredibly successful, and giving to the regular budget was on the rise. People were excited and enthusiastic about what they saw happening in their church. And then I received a phone call from the pastor. She was frustrated and angry because her leadership council was deadlocked over moving forward with several new ministries crucial to the church's vision for mission and ministry. There were two or three significant voices who regularly and routinely opposed moving forward and the leadership council was in stalemate, momentum was slowing, and the flame of revolution slowly dying. Can you guess my first question? Are they generous givers? I could almost see her wry smile as she said, "I knew you were going to ask that question so I checked and the answer is no." I said to my pastor, "You know what needs to happen, don't you?" She sighed and replied, "Yes, I guess I just needed to hear you say it." People who refuse to be generous, who refuse to tithe, who refuse to move forward with God's vision for the church, have no business being in positions of leadership.

In 1979, when Michael Slaughter was appointed to Ginhamsburg, average worship attendance was around ninety. Currently, there are around five thousand people in attendance on the various Ginghamsburg locations. (See Ginghamsburg website, http://ginghamsburg.org/bring/who-we-are /history.) In his book *Money Matters*, he states, "The selection of faithful, effective leaders is one of the most critical functions of ministry. . . . The pastor must make leadership selection and development one of the first priorities of her or his strategic plan." Most of us are probably nodding our heads in agreement at this point. But now it gets really interesting. He goes on to say,

It is absolutely essential that we place no one in a leadership position who is not both filled with God's spirit and faithful in stewardship. . . . When I first came to my congregation, I found godfathers and godmothers who sat on the board threatening to quit giving if I continued to press for change. But they were giving next to nothing. Guess what? They did quit giving, but at the end of the year the total offerings of the church increased. I have seen this happen again and again when churches quit operating out of fear and begin to appoint leaders and leadership boards based on sound biblical faithfulness.[9]

For Michael Slaughter, "sound biblical faithfulness" means tithing. Put as simply as possible, leaders need to be tithing and if they are not tithing or refuse to grow toward tithing, they should not be in positions of leadership. "Consider who might currently be on your leadership team who is not willing to grow, thus needing to be tactfully removed."[10]

One first step toward *tactfully removing* entrenched leadership is to utilize the Generosity Declaration you created, signed, and presented at worship. Doesn't it make sense to ask your leadership team to sign the Generosity Declaration? If a leader will not sign the Generosity Declaration they, in effect, have removed themselves from leadership. You, as pastor, need the courage to call them on it. "Remember that your church will never go beyond your leadership team."[11]

Recently, after leading a workshop I was approached by a local church stewardship chair. I could tell he was deeply troubled and needed to talk. We stepped aside and he very quietly and with a halting voice asked, "What do I do, Scott, if I know my pastor isn't on the giving list?" After taking a deep breath, I asked him, "Do you have a good relationship with your pastor?" When he replied yes, I then said, "You are going to have to sit down with your pastor and have one of the most difficult conversations you have ever had. You need to sit down and tell him you are concerned for his ministry and for the stewardship ministry of the church. Without his active support and leadership by example, the generosity revolution will fail before it ever starts. Then ask, how can I help you? I could tell by his nodding head that he knew in advance my response; he just needed encouragement and affirmation. If I want my pastor to succeed and help lead the revolution, then I might consider offering to pay for a session with a Christian financial planner. I may offer to pay for David Ramsey's Financial Peace University, with the proviso that my pastor and spouse attend. Listen, offer encouragement, and offer help. And just maybe sometime in the future, your pastor will have an incredible stewardship journey to share with your congrega-

---

9. Michael Slaughter with Kim Miller, *Money Matters: Financial Freedom for All God's Churches* (Nashville: Abingdon Press, 2006), 37.

10. Ibid., 39.

11. Ibid.

tion. If your revolution is going to be more than just a short-term uprising, your leadership must lead by example.

Once leadership steps up to lead the revolution in generosity, the next step must be to set new member expectations. By setting new member expectations regarding giving and tithing, you are nurturing the next generation of leaders. Contrary to other mainline churches, Ginghamsburg actually has more people attending than are on the membership rolls. Only one-third of the people attending Ginghamsburg are actual members.[12] Ginghamsburg requires new members to participate in a thirteen-week new members' class.[13] At the end of the class new members are expected to commit to four areas: participation in worship, connection to a small group, a place of service, and a commitment to tithing or commitment to a plan to get to tithing.[14]

Truthfully, you may not be able to do much about the many people on your rolls who currently do not take their membership vows seriously. You can, however, raise the expectation level for your leaders and then begin creating high-level expectations for your new members. High expectations for leadership and high expectations for your new members will insure the success of your revolution in generosity.

Don't Forget God

Expectations, vision, new member classes, giving kiosks and QR codes, thank-you notes, and telling stories will indeed fan the flame of your generosity revolution. However, never forget the greatest advantage the church has over most nonprofits—God! One of the members of my leadership team in a large midwestern church was a professional development officer for a local community college and also volunteered her time to help other nonprofits raise money. After one of our team meetings, she asked to speak with me privately. She asked, "What do you want me to give to the campaign?" And then she said, "Don't give me the nonsense of prayer and asking God. Tell me what I should pledge. That's the way we do it in my line of work." I half-jokingly responded, "I can't, because the truth of the matter is God probably has a lot higher number for you than I do." Too often, we focus so much on techniques, programs, and numbers that we forget God. We scour Amazon looking for the perfect book or resource and forget our

---

12. Ibid.

13. Sheryl Douglas and Carolyn Slaughter, *A Follower's Life* (Loveland, CO: Group Publications, 2002).

14. Slaughter with Miller, *Money Matters*, 40.

number one resource—God. Every discussion about generosity and giving needs to be surrounded and immersed with opportunities for prayer and cultivating our relationship with God. When we surround stewardship campaigns with opportunities for prayer, they become opportunities for transformation, not just ways to increase giving. Do you recall the quote on prayer from Henri Nouwen? "Prayer is the radical starting point of fundraising because in prayer we slowly experience a reorientation of all our thoughts and feelings about ourselves and others."[15]

Prayer changes the focus from me and what I want, to God and what God wants. The Horizons' campaign prayer of *Lord, what do you want to do through me?* may be the single most important part of any stewardship campaign. In the midst of campaigns I hear stories of marriages renewed, people called to ministry, career changes, and of course, people giving away more money than they ever could imagine—all because of daring to pray, *Lord, what do you want to do through me?*

Let me share with you portions of an e-mail I recently received from a participant in one of my stewardship campaigns.

As I was praying *Lord what do you want to do though me* and listening, I had the following financial things happen:

1. I received a notice that my employee portion of my health insurance premiums would increase a minimum of $250/month, plus I would lose dental and vision.

2. My local school taxes were being raised over $50 a month to help build a new school.

So, all of sudden I was faced with $300 in additional expenses per month. As someone who works for a nonprofit, this was huge. I knew God wanted me to increase my weekly giving, but I saw no way I could that and make an additional pledge to the capital campaign. So, I re-read our 21 Day Devotional guide, continued to pray, and spent time listening. Yesterday, I took the card and put down an amount I felt God was guiding me towards. I signed it, sealed the envelope, and laid it on the counter, preparing to take it to church the next day.

When I woke up this morning I checked my e-mail and found another e-mail from our company CFO. I figured great, another increase! God must

---

15. Henri Nouwen, *The Spirituality of Fundraising,* ed. John S. Mogabgab (Nashville: Upper Room, 2010), 34.

have laughed. Here our CFO was informing us that our monthly premium is increasing by just $15/month! And, this includes not only my health insurance but also my dental and vision care!

GOD IS AMAZING! Tears fill my eyes as I type this. Once again I have witnessed the powerful results of prayer and faith!

Yes, tithing charts and step-up charts can be helpful tools in helping cultivate generosity, but God has been and always will be the real change agent of the heart. Here are some suggestions for making sure we don't forget God.

Suggestions for Remembering God

1. Multiple times a year, not just during an annual campaign, invite people to prayerfully consider what they give and how they serve. Put a 3x5 card in the bulletin that says, *I am willing to pray daily for____ days about my giving and service to God.* Invite them to sign the card and bring it forward. As they come forward, hand them a 14- or 21-Day Devotional Guide. You might also consider handing out a prayer reminder at the same time. You could give out anything from a refrigerator magnet to a cardboard tent placard or a key fob. At the end of the time period invite people to respond with another card that says, *As a result of prayer I am going to...*

   - Do we?_____
     Can we?_____

2. Give people the opportunity to give witness to how God moved in their lives. As soon as I received the above-mentioned e-mail I told the pastor, "Ask this person to share this during worship."

   - Do we?_____
     Can we?_____

3. When you do have an annual campaign, make sure you include prayer vigils or prayer exercises before and at the

63

conclusion of the campaign. E-mail a daily devotion during the campaign to the congregation. Post the devotional on Facebook and encourage people to respond with insights and thoughts.

- Do we?_____
  Can we?_____

4. You might even use a generosity campaign to teach and encourage people to fast one day a week.

- Do we?_____
  Can we?_____

5. Ask your shut-ins to be in prayer for the congregation during your campaign. Sign them up for specific days or hours of prayer.

- Do we?_____
  Can we?_____

If you go to my website at www.scottmckenziegratitude.com you will find devotional guides and other prayer helps. Don't forget God!

A Yearlong Plan for Revolution

The plans of the diligent end up in profit,
but those who hurry end up with loss.

Prov 21:5 CEB

By their wisdom the prudent understand their way, but the stupidity of
fools deceives them.

Prov 14:8 CEB

You have recruited and trained your team of revolutionaries. You get the big picture and you have named the enemy. You are now aware of the keys that will fan the flame of revolution. The next step is to put this all together in a yearlong plan for revolution. No two revolutions are alike. To effectively plan your year of revolution, you need to know your weaknesses as well as your own positions of strength. A Generosity Survey will be a great place to start. Print off the following survey for your team to fill out prior to your stewardship retreat. Your team will spend time together discussing and evaluating each question. Your response to the survey will help you create a twelve-month Generosity Plan.

Generosity Survey

1. Does your pastor know who gives and how much?

    (1) Knows nothing, wants to know nothing

(2) Wants to know but is denied access

(3) Has some idea and is given some information

(4) Has full access

2. Does your pastor tithe and share his story with your congregation?

(1) No, and never talks about money

(2) We think so, but he won't talk about it

(3) Yes, and will talk about it in a general sense

(4) Yes, talks about freely and openly, even talks amounts

3. Does your pastor talk about finances and giving?

(1) Can't remember the last time

(2) For two or three weeks but only during a financial campaign

(3) Regularly and throughout the year

4. When a person is asked to serve in a leadership role, is his or her giving taken into consideration?

(1) We would never do something like that

(2) Our pastor might make reference to it

(3) Yes, we take seriously a person's generosity and giving when filling leadership positions in our church

5. Do you expect your leaders to either tithe or work toward a tithe?

(1) No expectation or discussion about giving and leadership

(2) We encourage it but that's about it

(3) Leaders are expected to be tithing or move toward tithing

6. Do your leaders give witness to their giving and why they give?

(1) Never

(2) Yes, but never anything very specific

(3) On a regular basis and on specific topics (tithing, electronic giving, debt, and so on)

7. Do laypeople other than leaders give witness to their giving?

(1) Never

(2) Only during our financial campaign

(3) Regularly and year-round

8. Do you regularly tell stories of how your ministries change lives?

    (1) In worship _____yes _____no

    (2) In newsletters _____yes _____no

    (3) In giving statements _____yes _____no

    (4) In e-mail blasts _____yes _____no

9. Are children and youth regularly taught stewardship and encouraged to give?

    (1) Giving banks _____yes _____no

    (2) Offering envelopes _____yes _____no

    (3) Lessons on tithing _____yes _____no

10. Are your children and youth asked to give witness to what the church means to them?

    (1) Never

    (2) Only during our financial campaign

    (3) Regularly and year-round

11. Does your church have a unique vision for ministry that unites your congregation and sets you apart from other churches?

    (1) No

    (2) Our pastor might

    (3) Yes, but we really aren't united around it

    (4) Yes, and it drives everything we do as a church

12. Do you challenge people to increase their giving or step toward tithing?

    (1) Seldom, if ever

    (2) Only during a financial campaign

    (3) Regularly throughout the year

13. Do new members attend a class and agree to either tithe or work toward a tithe?

    (1) No classes and no expectations

    (2) We have a class but no real discussion/teaching about giving/tithing

    (3) We have a class with discussion/teaching about giving/tithing but no real expectation

(4) We discuss/teach and have clearly stated expectations for new members about giving/tithing

14. When it comes to statements of giving:

    (1) We only send a year-end tax statement
    (2) We send one out two or three times a year but generic with only difference being the amount
    (3) We include a thank-you and ministry story
    (4) We send different letters to different groups of givers

15. Do people have opportunity to give through:

    (1) Boxed envelopes passed out once a year
    (2) Monthly or quarterly mailed envelopes
    (3) Envelopes plus _____ kiosks _____ online _____QR codes _____electronic/automatic ___website

16. Do you regularly thank your pledgers and your givers? _____yes _____no

17. Do you find special ways to thank the top 20 percent of your givers? _____yes _____no

18. Do you clearly connect prayer and faith with financial giving through the use of prayer vigils, prayer walks, fasting, or use of devotional guides? _____yes _____no

19. Do you have an endowment fund? _____yes _____no

20. Can endowment income be used for routine operating expenses? _____yes _____no

21. Do you have a plan in place to grow your endowment?

    _____ brochures _____ a legacy society _____ celebrate and acknowledge legacy gifts

Generosity Planning Retreat

The next step is a retreat with the Generosity Team and Staff. The objective of the retreat is threefold:

1. Review and discuss the Generosity Declaration and its significance for the team members.

2. Review the results of your Generosity Survey and the four questions listed above.

3. Create a twelve-month plan for insuring the success of your generosity revolution.

At your retreat begin with a review of your Generosity Declaration. Ask for discussion around the following questions:

1. What part of the Declaration has had the biggest impact on your life?

2. Has it changed how you live your life in any way?

3. What has proved to be the most difficult or challenging aspect of the Declaration?

4. Is there something in particular that you need prayer for or help with as we move forward as a Generosity team?

Now begin to review the results of your survey and your responses to these questions:

1. What are our areas of strength?

2. What are our glaring weaknesses and deficiencies?

3. What are some quick and easy fixes we can easily implement?

4. What are the long-term issues we need to consider?

Create Your 12-Month Plan

Next, take the following chart or a 12-month calendar and begin to fill it out. Do not attempt to do everything in the first year. Be strategic and just get started. Remember, whatever you do is going to be more than what has been done in the past. Incorporate additional ideas next year. Here are the generosity issues you want to insure are included in your long-term generosity plan:

- Preaching and teaching

- Giving witness to generosity
- Telling stories of changed lives
- Saying thank you
- Including children and youth
- Not forgetting God
- Developing clear expectation for leaders and new members
- Creating a variety of giving opportunities
- Personal financial management
- Communication pieces with a focus on gratitude and ministry

Sample A of a 12-Month Planning Chart

Generosity Activity	September (focus on children)	October	November	December
Preaching	Parents train their children in generosity and giving	Series for annual campaign (if held in fall)	Conclusion of annual campaign	The Greatest Gift. Our response
Tell Stories of Changed Lives (Worship, video, e-mails)	Young person give witness to what church has meant to them. Someone who has been through Financial Peace	Lay witness as part of the campaign	Invite someone to give witness as to why they are giving a legacy gift	A video of the past year and what ministry has occurred
Say Thank You Quarterly statements	Quarterly statement with a story about children or youth ministry, maybe VBS		To those who have gone on before us. All Saints' Day—legacy giving	Thank-you notes to everyone who made a pledge during the campaign. Quarterly statement—Thank you and ministry story

Children and Youth	Give out children's giving banks. Dave Ramsey.com	Children and youth stewardship studies	Invite children and youth to participate in the campaign	Special Christmas offering for others
Don't Forget God	Special prayer time for children and parents. Consider a commitment time for parents and modeling their giving	Prayer vigil and devotional guides as part of the campaign		
Set Expectations Leaders and New Members	Ask pastor to begin considering potential leaders and their history of giving	New members' class. Teaching on tithing and expectations	When nominating new leaders have clearly stated expectations	
Giving Opportunities		Have leadership give witness to use of electronic giving	On All Saints' Day focus on legacy giving. Kickoff legacy society with a banquet	Have a QR code in the bulletin for a special Christmas offering. Show people how to use it

Personal Financial Management	Begin advertising Financial Peace University or some other personal finance teaching	Begin Financial Peace or other study		Have an emphasis on a simple Christmas and avoiding debt
Misc.	Begin putting together a ministry- or mission-focused budget		Present ministry budget *not* a line-item budget	

Generosity Activity	January	February	March	April
Preaching	Vision for ministry and mission in the coming year	Begin preparing congregation for Lenten trial tithe	Spiritual disciplines, including generosity	Stewardship of earth
Tell Stories of Changed Lives (worship, video, e-mails)	Witness from a life impacted by ministry	Older married couple give witness to a lifetime of tithing	Witness to the power of spiritual disciplines	Video compilation of people who have experienced change and new life
Say Thank You Quarterly statements	Year-end statements that also say thank you and provide pictures and stories of ministry. Make this comprehensive.	Thank You Banquet for those who gave $1,000 or more	Quarterly statement thank you and ministry story	Church-wide first-quarter update on financial status. Focus on ministries
Children and Youth		Confirmation class: tithing and service	Special children and youth lent/Easter giving	Special children and youth earth day service project

Don't Forget God	A litany of thanksgiving for all that occurred in previous year	At every leadership meeting for the entire year have a candle or another symbol repre-senting presence of Christ	Opportu-nities to commit to spiritual disciplines	Commitment card for steward-ship of earth
Set Expecta-tions Lead-ers and New Members	Present new leaders and have them publically commit to the leadership covenant		New members' class. Teaching on tithing and expec-tations	
Giving Op-portunities	Share the number of families that have signed up for elec-tronic giving. Send them a special thank you.		QR code in bulletin for a spe-cial Easter offering	Send your video compilation out as an e-mail with a prominent "Give" button.
Personal Financial Manage-ment		Three-week debt-reduction class		
Misc.			Congrega-tion-wide book study on priorities or spiritual disciplines	Ministry Fair

Generosity Activity	May	June	July	August
Preaching	Mother's Day and Memorial Day sacrificial giving	Giving of time and service. With ministry fair. Spiritual gifts		
Tell Stories of Changed Lives (worship, video, e-mails)	Multi-generation mother-daughter witness. Veteran witness	Youth / Confirmation class witness Witness on why I include church in my will		
Say Thank You Quarterly statements		Quarterly statement thank-you and ministry story. Encouragement for summer giving		Thank you to VBS workers. Video e-mail about VBS with a "Give" button

Children and Youth	Exercise on parable of the talents	Celebrate and witness the results from parable of the talents		
Don't Forget God		Prayer focus on *Lord, what do you want from me regarding service?*		
Set Expectations Leaders and New Members		Check up for leadership and faithfulness to the covenant. What do they struggle with? Where do they need help? Celebrate areas of growth and change		Picnic/gathering for all new members during year. Opportunity to make sure they are connected

Giving Opportunities		Video e-mail about electronic giving during summer. A link to sign up	Evaluate your electronic giving process, website giving. Check for ease of use. Begin preparing for a trial period of giving kiosk using iPads	
Personal Financial Management		Wills Workshop with special invitations		Begin preparing for Financial Peace
Misc.		Spiritual gifts inventory class		Review church newsletters, bulletins, website, and other communications to be sure they reflect gratitude, abundance, and ministry

Sample A of a 12-Month Planning Chart

Here is a sample calendar for how you can make stewardship a priority year-round:

Month	Activity
January	Year-End statements—Be sure to send a year-end statement to all who made a gift to your church (pledgers and non-pledgers). Obviously this is needed for tax purposes, but it also provides an opportunity to say thank you to those who are supporting your ministry. Let them know how their gifts were put to good use. Let them know what you intend to do with their generous donations in the new year. Annual Meeting—At the annual meeting of your congregation, frequently the finance chair is asked to present the line-item budget to the congregation and then ask for questions. Droning on about increasing healthcare costs and gas prices, the finance chair garners very little enthusiasm about bountiful giving! Is it any wonder these meetings are often poorly attended? You can still have the line-item budget available for those who want to see it (almost no one will), but try presenting a ministry-focused budget instead. Talk about your vibrant ministries and all the ways you are serving your community. Proportion your budget into ministry categories (Worship, Pastoral Care, Christian Education, Communication, and Outreach) based on the amount of resources spent in each area. For example, clergy in a pastoral-size church may distribute costs related to her position as 50 percent worship (sermon preparation, working with musicians, and so on), 25 percent pastoral care (hospital visits, marriage counseling), 10 percent Christian education (adult education classes and confirmation), 10 percent communication (writing for newsletter, visitor contacts), and 5 percent outreach (supporting food pantry, Kiwanis). Creating a ministry-focused budget is not an exact science, but your end result should reflect the amount of ministry that is being supported by the donations made by your members. Include one stewardship witness in worship sometime in January.

February	Recruit new stewardship committee members and organize a retreat to plan for the year. Review results of fall stewardship process. Consider how your process could be improved. During your retreat, be sure to include time for prayer, reflection, Bible study, and stewardship education. Be sure to open up conversations about money. Invite members to share their own stewardship experiences and where they are on their journeys. You may want to use this time to create a statement of stewardship describing what your stewardship committee believes about giving and generosity. Include one stewardship witness in worship sometime in February.
March	New Member Class—During the new member class, be sure to clearly articulate your church's vision for ministry and how you plan to accomplish it. Teach about stewardship as grounded in gratitude, revealed in prayer, and lived in faith. Provide an opportunity for new members to participate in giving through a pledge card, electronic giving, or another vehicle. You may want to include some prayer support for discerning their giving such as a devotional book, stewardship prayers, or a list of scriptures that relate to stewardship. Lent is a great time for prayer and reflection. Be sure your materials include the prayerful discernment of God's will for all our resources. Include one stewardship witness in worship during March.
April	Send quarterly statements—include a thank-you for gifts received and a description of what has been accomplished; be sure to include information on what you intend to accomplish next with the gifts of your congregation. Promote your "wish list" to the congregation. This is a list of projects or needs that fall outside the annual budget but are a part of achieving your vision for ministry. Make sure you complete the "ask" by letting people know how much it will cost and to whom they should speak about making the gift. Include one stewardship witness in worship during April.

May	Planned Giving—Host a workshop on estates and wills and invite the entire congregation. Although the average age for a person creating their first will is forty, most people in the United States die without a will or estate plan. Invite a local expert to encourage people to create a simple will. Be sure to also provide language that enables someone to easily include your church in their will either as sole beneficiary, partial beneficiary (dollar amount or percent), or beneficiary contingent on the death of other heirs. If you don't already have one, establish an endowment fund. We recommend you create an endowment fund with a specified purpose before receiving a large gift, rather than after when it is likely to cause some conflict. Begin a new tradition of providing fourth graders with banks with three sections—Save/Spend/Share (available from various resources online). Include one stewardship witness in worship during May.
June	Time and Talent—This is a great time to identify new leadership in preparation for the ramping up for the fall programming. Host an adult forum on spiritual gifts, possibly completing a spiritual gifts inventory form. Prepare a list of ministry areas within the church along with current leadership and contact information. Ask members to consider how they may use their spiritual gifts in support of the ministries of your church. You may wish to have them complete a pledge card indicating their areas of interest. If someone completes a card and indicates interest, it is vitally important they are asked to serve. So often we have heard about time and talent surveys that were taken and volunteers were never called to serve. Include one stewardship witness in worship during June.

July	Send quarterly statements
	Be sure that thank-you notes are being written; now is also a good time to send thank-you notes to those who have been involved in leadership or served the church in significant ways.
	Online and Electronic Giving—Review your processes for online and electronic giving through EFTs. Test it out and be sure it is user friendly and convenient. Promote this opportunity to the congregation, providing testimony from those who are giving electronically.
	Include one stewardship witness in worship during July.
August	Review your communication materials. What do they say to an outsider about your church's priorities? Do they say, "Our costs are up and we need more money" or do they say, "We are a thriving community doing transformational ministry and mission." Review church newsletters, bulletins, website, and other communications to be sure they reflect gratitude, abundance, ministry, and mission.
	Include one stewardship witness in worship during August.
September	New Member Class
	Include one stewardship witness in worship in September.

October	Send quarterly statements—This will be timed so that members are reminded of the amount of their pledges just prior to the launch of the annual financial appeal.
	Financial Stewardship process—seven weeks Sunday One—Pastor shares stewardship witness 　　　　　　Distribute devotional guide to congregation 　　　　　　and invite them to be in prayer
	Sunday Two—Gratitude Sunday Pastor preaches on God as the source of all gifts; distribute index cards that say "I am grateful to God for…" and ask people to complete them in worship. Following Gratitude Sunday, display gratitude cards in a high-traffic area so people will see them throughout the week. Lay stewardship witness in worship
	Sunday Three—Cardboard testimonies; have members share their witness via cardboard testimonies in worship
November	Sunday Four—Lay stewardship witness in worship Commitment Sunday—pledge cards distributed, collected, and offered as an act of worship
	Sunday Five—One more opportunity to complete and offer pledge cards Monday after Sunday Five—Send letter inviting those who have not yet made a pledge to do so; include pledge card and return addressed envelope
	Sunday Six—One last opportunity to complete and offer pledge cards Week after Sunday Six—make contacts with those who have not yet made a pledge
	Sunday Seven—Celebrate results and give thanks

December	Mail confirmation letters to those who pledged with a note of thanks. Church leadership should write thank-you notes to all who made a pledge. Pastor should write thank-you notes to those who are providing substantial support, those who increased substantially, and others who appear to be giving sacrificially.

Close Your Retreat

Conclude your retreat with

- Communion
- Reaffirmation of your Generosity Declaration
- Dedication of the Annual Plans

Conclusion

Don't remember the prior things; don't ponder ancient history. Look! I'm
doing a new thing; now it sprouts up; don't you recognize it? I'm making
a way in the desert, paths in the wilderness.

Isa 43:18-19 CEB

I live in hope. Yes, I know the numbers are bad when it comes to giving in so many of our churches and denominations. Yes, I know we face a huge challenge in our culture, as people continue to love their stuff more than they love God. But I also see the seeds of revolution beginning to root and grow. Generosity is rising; lone nuts are, by God's grace, becoming revolutionary leaders. Pastor Doug and his wife Dee are two such leaders. Doug and Dee have faithfully danced in the middle of the field, often by themselves, wondering if they would always be two lone nuts. They have done this dance in small and medium-sized churches throughout central Pennsylvania. With their permission let me share with you excerpts of their stewardship story.

We were humbled when we counted up that this will be our seventh campaign and our fourth in the last six years. As pastor and leader of other churches over the past twenty-three years, we have invested in ministry and a vision of a brighter future and gave up investing in a retirement home and so much more. We stepped out in faith believing we could never out give God and have never been disappointed.

Dee and I understood that if God's vision and mission was to be accomplished at our church, we were going to have to step up and lead the way. What was God asking us to do?

I'll be honest—we're still wrestling with God, but the number right now is a second tithe—that we will invest in our church an additional 10 percent for the next three years. Is that enough after all God has blessed Dee and I with all these years?

85

I want you to understand that for us that is a huge amount. Dee the pragmatist immediately asked, "How will we do it?" We prayed, we talked, and a plan began to emerge. We've learned in our twenty-four years together that God will provide. Will you step out with us and sacrificially make a gift that reflects how God has blessed you and put your trust in God that he will continue to provide for all of us?

People came and joined Dee and Doug in the dance of generosity. Generosity indeed began to rise and a revolution began to take hold. Read Doug's own words as he described what happened.

> What happened here is nothing short of miraculous.... What happened was a spiritual renewal that awoke a sleeping giant.... Scott helped us tell our story, stir the hearts of many and remind us of why we exist as the church. While it was never about money, we set the goal at $350,000.00 to retire a building debt and replace the sanctuary roof. When the final figures were in we had pledges of over $466,000.00.... Once our stated goals are met, we will be able to re-establish a capital improvement/reserve fund and expand our mission endeavors.

Clearly, revolution is possible. Yes, year-round stewardship is important. Yes, I believe in leadership covenants, vision statements, and generosity job descriptions. Yes, I believe in giving kiosks, online giving, and thank-you notes. But in the end, I believe in the fundamental importance of revolutionary leaders who are willing to ask themselves these critical questions:

- Am I willing to be the kind of revolutionary leader exemplified by Jesus?
- Am I willing to risk being a lone nut?
- Do I really believe in the glorious vision of our Generosity Declaration: that all people are created in the image of a loving, giving, and generous God?
- Do I believe that generosity and stewardship are a novel journey of surpassing importance—the journey of becoming the people God created us to be from the beginning of all creation?

Please join me in prayer as we begin this glorious revolution.

All-loving and all-giving God, grant me the courage to be a revolutionary leader on behalf of your kingdom. When I become weary of being the lone nut, dancing by myself, remind me of this novel journey of surpassing importance. Help me, oh God, to live a life of gratitude, prayer, and faith as I bear witness to your love, grace, and generosity. Amen.

Let the Revolution begin!

The 21-Day Challenge

Day One

Scripture—Genesis 1:1-2 THE MESSAGE

First this: God created the Heavens and Earth—all you see, all you don't see. Earth was a soup of nothingness, a bottomless emptiness, an inky blackness. God's Spirit brooded like a bird above the watery abyss.

Reflection

I love to read. I will usually read at least one book a week: Christian, fiction, suspense, nonfiction, history, pretty much everything. Yesterday, I decided to give up that reading and only read the Bible. I am hoping to make it through most of the Bible in the forty days of Lent.

In an attempt to read with new eyes I am using THE MESSAGE translation. Reading them in THE MESSAGE, those first familiar verses in Genesis struck me in an entirely new way. Perhaps the most important words in all of scripture are the first three words. First this: God. First this: God. In order for my life to make sense, First this: God. Without God being first, life is a soup of nothingness, a bottomless emptiness, an inky blackness. There is good news, my friends. In the midst of nothingness, bottomless emptiness, and inky blackness God is ever present. God is present, and God is always working to bring new life and creation into my soup of nothingness, my bottomless emptiness, and my inky blackness.

First this: God. Truth be told, when I find myself in that place of nothingness, emptiness, and blackness I have often put something or someone other than God in first place. Like Lent, a stewardship effort can be a glorious invitation to reexamine our lives and spend, in this case, twenty-one days of putting God first. The promise is, as we put God first, there will be a new creation; a soup of nothingness becomes a feast of abundance, bottomless emptiness becomes joyful satisfaction, and inky blackness transforms into a brilliant light of love and hope.

Will you join me on a twenty-one-day journey of First this: God?

Prayer

Thank you, God, for the amazing story of creation. Thank you for your continuing creation in my life. Help me over these next twenty-one days to put you first. Amen.

Day Two

Scripture—Hosea 14:3 CEB

Assyria won't save us; we won't ride upon horses; we will no longer say, "Our God," to the work of our hands. In you the orphan finds compassion.

Reflection

Tears streamed down Susan's face as she stood before the congregation and shared her stewardship story. Susan is a physician who literally came up the hard way. Susan's mother was bipolar and self-medicated with drugs and alcohol. As an infant, Susan was often rescued from bars and street corners by aunts and uncles. Susan survived. Against all odds she went to college and onto medical school. She successfully completed her residency as the first African-American female in the program. Susan now has her own very successful practice. If anyone ever had the right to say they were a self-made man or woman it would be Susan.

And yet, as I heard Susan tell her story, it was never about Susan but always about gratitude, and always about God. Susan recognized that it was the hand of God that had saved her, not her own. Susan somehow knew that everything she had was a gift, a gift from the hand of a loving and compassionate God. Because Susan realized everything was a gift, she gave back in amazingly generous ways.

Take a moment and look at your hands. Are these the hands that have created your life? Are these the hands that have made you successful? Is your life and all that you have and all you have accomplished the work of these hands? In gazing at your own hands can you somehow see the hand of God? Right now as you gaze at your hands, say, "Thank you, oh God, for all that I am and all that I have are the result of your hands. Thank you!"

Prayer

Oh God, I confess it is so very easy to look at my hands and think of all that I have accomplished and done. Help me, oh God, to see your hands. Help me, oh God, to recognize you as the source of all I have and all that I am. And help me to give back in gratitude. Thank you, God!

Day Three

Scripture—Luke 17:15-19 CEB

One of them, when he saw that he had been healed, returned and praised God with a loud voice. He fell on his face at Jesus' feet and thanked him. He was a Samaritan. Jesus replied, "Weren't ten cleansed? Where are the other nine? No one returned to praise God except this foreigner?" Then Jesus said to him, "Get up and go. Your faith has healed you."

Reflection

Ten lepers healed by Jesus and only one returns to give thanks. Make no mistake, they were all physically healed of their disease. Their wish, their dream, had come true. But only one returned to give thanks. And in giving thanks, real thanks, Jesus says to this one leper, "Your faith has healed you."

But wait a minute, he had already been healed. Maybe, just maybe, there is a healing that goes far beyond the physical. Maybe, just maybe, real healing of heart and soul only occurs when we are truly grateful, when our hearts overflow with thanksgiving as we recognize God as the source of all we have and all we are. We can have our prayers answered, our dreams fulfilled, and still not be truly whole and happy until we return to God with gratitude. Maybe, just maybe, we could dare to change Jesus' words to the tenth leper and say, "Get up and on your way, your gratitude has healed and saved you."

I wonder, how much of what ails our churches, our pastors, and our leaders could be healed with an outpouring of gratitude. What if our churches were thankful for what they have instead of what they lack? What might happen if we would begin expressing gratitude on a regular basis to our leaders and members? What might happen if church members began writing notes of gratitude to pastors? What if all the energy we put into asking for money and time was also put into saying thank you? Maybe, just maybe, there could be a healing of heart and soul; a life lived in joyful abundance.

Today, I invite each of us to return to God in gratitude and thankfulness. Hear now these words of Jesus for you. "Get up and on your way, your gratitude has healed and saved you."

Prayer

Oh God, you have given me so much. And so often I forget to return and give you thanks. Thank you for all you have done for me, for all the precious gifts you have so graciously given me. Thank you. And now with faith and gratitude I go forth knowing you have healed me and saved me. Amen.

Day Four

Scripture—Psalm 118:24-26 ceb

This is the day the LORD acted;
   we will rejoice and celebrate in it!
LORD, please save us!
   LORD, please let us succeed!
The one who enters in the LORD's name is blessed;
   we bless all of you from the LORD's house.

Reflection

The more familiar translation of this scripture is, "This is the day the LORD has made, we will rejoice and be glad in it" (NKJV). In both versions there are no qualifiers: no ifs, ands, buts, or maybes. In *Jesus Calling*, Sara Young writes the following about these verses: "How precious are My children who remember to thank Me at all times. They can walk through the darkest days with Joy in their hearts because they know that the Light of My Presence is still shining on them."[1]

John has every reason in the world to be angry and resentful. By the world's standards life is not fair. His beloved wife suffers from cancer and he is her primary caregiver. And now John is in the early stages of Alzheimer's. What will he do? Who will take care of his beloved wife? And yet, as I share lunch in their modest home John's face is radiant with joy and peace. What is John's secret? John is one of those "precious children" described by Sara Young. John knows there are dark days ahead, but he knows and believes that the light of God's love and grace will always shine on him and his beloved. For John, every day is a gift because each day is full of God's presence, even in the midst of cancer and Alzheimer's. John knows what he and his beloved are facing; but he also knows who walks beside them each moment of every day. And he is thankful!

Do I know I am a precious child of God? Can I recall a time when I knew who was walking beside me? Am I angry? Am I resentful? Am I thankful?

---

1. Sarah Young, *Jesus Calling* (Dallas: Thomas Nelson, 2004), 345.

Prayer

Thank you, God, for people like John, who show me how to live. Help me to live today as one of your precious children. Help me to remember, oh God, that even as I walk in darkness, your light shines upon me; and I will give you thanks. Amen.

Day Five

Scripture—Colossians 4:2-4 CEB

Keep on praying and guard your prayers with thanksgiving. At the same time, pray for us also. Pray that God would open a door for the word so we can preach the secret plan of Christ—which is why I'm in chains. Pray that I might be able to make it as clear as I ought to when I preach.

Reflection

As I read the scripture for today I am instantly transported back to Malawi and the infamous Sun Village Inn. The Sun Village Inn was our hotel for one very long night. For no extra charge, the Sun Village Inn provided attacking wolf spiders, bats, bed bugs, holes in the ceilings, broken bathroom fixtures, and all the cold water you could use. Most of us "stayed alert with eyes wide open," but not in gratitude. Instead, our eyes were wide open in worry and fear.

The next morning as we gathered for breakfast, as spoiled, pampered Americans, we complained endlessly. In the midst of our whining and complaining we heard the small quiet voice of Sara, the niece of our interpreter. Sara told us she "saw the face of God" in her hotel room. You see, Sara's eyes were "wide open in gratitude" as she told us in all of her life she had never before slept in a bed. Needless to say, our complaining ceased.

My dear friends, head into today with your eyes wide open in gratitude. Look and search diligently, not for what might be wrong or a problem or something to complain about, but search diligently today for the face of God; look for ways to be grateful and you just might be surprised, even if you are staying in the Sun Village Inn.

Prayer

Oh God, forgive me for going through life with my eyes closed to all that you have given to me, to all of your blessings. Help me to live today with my eyes wide open in gratitude. Amen.

Day Six

Scripture—Philippians 4:4-6 CEB

Be glad in the Lord always! Again I say, be glad! Let your gentleness show in your treatment of all people. The Lord is near. Don't be anxious about anything; rather, bring up all of your requests to God in your prayers and petitions, along with giving thanks.

Reflection

Julie's life has not been easy. She was raised in scarcity and would take the change from the offering envelope just to get something to eat. Then, her only daughter at age twelve was stricken with leukemia and not expected to live. Julie herself has endured numerous surgeries just to be able to function and get around.

Now her church is having a capital campaign and she was asked to give. Her first response was, "No way." But as Julie spoke to our team she said, "Something strange began to happen as I asked myself, what do I have to be grateful for?" In spite of all her struggles Julie began to realize how God had blessed her and all the many reasons she had to be grateful. And with a smile on her face she spoke of an amazingly generous gift, a gift given with thanksgiving and great joy.

Today, we each will be faced with a choice. We can either look for things that are wrong and irritate us, or like Julie we can keep our "eyes wide open in gratitude."

Prayer

Dear God, it is so very easy for me to see all of the things wrong in my life, and all the things I don't have. Give me eyes wide open in gratitude and show me how to live and give. Amen.

Day Seven

Scripture—Matthew 20:15-16 CEB

"Don't I have the right to do what I want with what belongs to me? Or are you resentful because I'm generous?" So those who are last will be first. And those who are first will be last.

Reflection

Yes, Lord, I confess that sometimes when I look around at what other people have and how they have been blessed I am envious. Sometimes, Lord, you seem to answer the prayers of others so quickly and in such miraculous ways that I am jealous. While I muddle through the back roads of life trying to figure out which way to go, others seem to be on the superhighway of life, straight ahead, full speed, no detours or exits.

So what's the answer? The answer can be found in one of our earlier scriptures: "Keep on praying and guard your prayers with thanksgiving" (Col 4:2 CEB).

I can choose to focus on what I do not have, or I can choose to focus on what I do have. I can even in the midst of envy and jealousy make a choice to stay alert, with my eyes wide open in gratitude. And in the midst of having my eyes wide open in gratitude, a miracle slowly begins to occur: anger, jealousy, envy, and bitterness slowly fade away.

Prayer

Oh God, right now in this moment help me to stay alert and have my eyes wide open in gratitude. Whatever comes my way on this day, let me be grateful. Amen.

Day Eight

Scripture—2 Corinthians 8:1-2 CEB

> Brothers and sisters, we want to let you know about the grace of God that was given to the churches of Macedonia. While they were being tested by many problems, their extra amount of happiness and their extreme poverty resulted in a surplus of rich generosity.

Reflection

Sasha is a ten-year-old Russian orphan. When the church group I was with visited the orphanage, Sasha, for some reason, latched on to me. He took me by the arm and led me through the orphanage showing off his room and the place he ate meals. All the while Sasha's eyes were filled with joy and laughter. In spite of the fact I spoke little Russian and Sasha spoke no English, we connected. As we prepared to depart, Sasha sat beside me, pulled a silver ring from his finger, and held it out for me to take. My eyes filled with tears and I spoke the only Russian word I knew—"Nyet, nyet." (No, no.) This child, who had nothing in the world to call his own except this ring, desperately wanted to give the ring to me. When asked why he wanted to give his only possession away, Sasha responded, "Because I am so thankful you came." For Sasha, abundant joy, extreme poverty, and a heart filled with gratitude overflowed in a wealth of generosity.

For many of us who have so much, we want more. We are not thankful for what we have and always look for the "something more." And truth be told, it's never enough. What would happen if, by God's grace, our desire to gain more and have more could be transformed by gratitude into a heartfelt desire to give more? What would happen if in a spirit of gratitude, we spent as much time figuring out ways to give as we spend figuring out how to earn, have, and keep?

What are you most deeply grateful for? Can you recall a time when someone who could least afford it gave you a generous gift? What was it like? How did you respond? Did it affect you in any way? Does what you give in money, time, talent, and service reflect the depth of your gratitude?

Prayer

Oh God, thank you for the examples of gratitude and generosity you have sent into our lives. Forgive us, Lord, for being more concerned with how much we can earn, have, and keep, instead of being thankful for all we have. Forgive me for worrying about _____. Help me, God, to be truly grateful and abundantly generous. Amen.

Day Nine

Scripture—John 10:10 CEB

The thief enters only to steal, kill, and destroy. I came so that they could have life—indeed, so that they could live life to the fullest.

Reflection

His name is James and he is a walking, talking, breathing miracle. James is about twenty years old, and a few years ago, was in a serious automobile accident. James was declared dead at the scene. On the ride to the hospital he had a seizure and his heart started beating. While technically alive, James was in a deep coma with no real hope of recovery. The doctors told his parents there was a one-in-ten-million chance James would ever recover. Clearly, someone forgot to tell God. James will tell you that he met Jesus, who told him he could go back home to his family. James came back, slowly.

While James still has challenges to overcome, his face radiates joy. James is likely at any moment to break into a loud praise to God. Who can blame him? James reminds me that the abundant life is not found in the things that I own or the money that I make. The voices whispering in my ear, "Abundance is found in things or stuff" are the voices of robbers and thieves. James reminds me, the abundant life is simply a life filled with gratitude and joy for this moment, the only moment I truly have. How have I listened to the voices of the "robbers and thieves"? What does the abundant life mean to me?

Prayer

Oh God, far too often I listen to the voices of thieves and robbers whispering in my ear about what I need for the abundant life. Forgive me. Help me to live like Francis. Help me to live in this moment with gratitude, joy, and faith. Amen.

Day Ten

Scripture—Luke 6:12-16 CEB

> During that time, Jesus went out to the mountain to pray, and he prayed to God all night long. At daybreak, he called together his disciples. He chose twelve of them whom he called apostles: Simon, whom he named Peter; his brother Andrew; James; John…Matthew…Judas Iscariot, who became a traitor.

Reflection

In preparation for one of his most important decisions, Jesus spends the night in prayer. And frankly, the results are not very impressive or inspiring. After a night of prayer Jesus chooses a hot-headed, impulsive Peter; a despised tax collector named Matthew; Judas, who would betray him; and two brothers, James and John, whose primary concern was who would be the greatest.

When facing important decisions, how many of us have used the time-honored tradition of making two columns on a sheet of paper, one column for the pluses and one column for the minuses? Look at the list and then make your decision. Let me tell you, if Jesus had done that, he never would have chosen this bunch!

Bob kept looking at the spreadsheet and the spreadsheet said one number, but his prayer, "Lord, what do you want to do through me?" was clearly giving a very different answer. Then he received word that his insurance was going up by nearly three hundred dollars a month. Now, his spreadsheet was screaming, "DON'T." After another sleepless night of prayer he filled out his card with fear and trepidation. He had listened to God and not the spreadsheet. The very next day, Bob received an e-mail from his company informing him there had been a mistake and insurance was only going up twenty dollars a month. Tears filled Bob's eyes as he read the e-mail over and over again, overwhelmed with the goodness and grace of God.

Now friends, there is nothing wrong with lists and spreadsheets, but let's not ignore our greatest gift and asset, prayer. Are you facing important decisions? Turn to God in prayer. Ask for guidance. Dare to pray, "Lord, what would you do through me?"

Prayer

Oh God, help me to turn to you in prayer for guidance and direction. Give me the courage to ask, the faith to believe, and the will to act. Amen.

Day Eleven

Scripture—John 4:46-50 CEB

In Capernaum there was a certain royal official whose son was sick. When he heard that Jesus was coming from Judea to Galilee, he went out to meet him and asked Jesus if he would come and heal his son, for his son was about to die. Jesus said to him, "Unless you see miraculous signs and wonders, you won't believe." The royal official said to him, "Lord, come before my son dies." Jesus replied, "Go home. Your son lives." The man believed the word that Jesus spoke to him and set out for his home.

Reflection

I don't know how or why this prayer thing works. But I do know that Jesus tells several parables or stories concerning the power of persistence in prayer. As Americans, we like everything now. When I have a question, any question, I go to Google and within seconds have my answer. Oh if God was like Google!! But for some reason it doesn't work that way.

Monica was the mother of Augustine, one of the greatest writers and thinkers of the early church. Eventually, Augustine became a bishop. In his younger days, Augustine would have nothing to do with God, didn't need God. Augustine was brilliant and evidently had quite a way with women, many women. Monica, his saintly mother, prayed every day for his conversion. After years of pleading and crying to God, her prayers were answered. Augustine was baptized at age thirty-two and one year later Monica died, a happy woman and mother.

Today's word: persistent. Don't give up in prayer.

Today, who needs you to lift them up in prayer? What miracle just might happen because you are persistent in prayer? What miracles may have happened in your life because of others praying for you? Give thanks to God and be persistent in prayer.

Prayer

Oh God, I fall on my knees with gratitude for the unknown people who have been praying for me. I thank you for answered prayer. Show me someone today in need of my prayers. Help me to be persistent. Help me to believe. Amen.

Day Twelve

Scripture—Genesis 32:24-28 CEB

But Jacob stayed apart by himself, and a man wrestled with him until dawn broke. When the man saw that he couldn't defeat Jacob, he grabbed Jacob's thigh and tore a muscle in Jacob's thigh as he wrestled with him. The man said, "Let me go because the dawn is breaking." But Jacob said, "I won't let you go until you bless me." He said to Jacob, "What's your name?" and he said, "Jacob." Then he said, "Your name won't be Jacob any longer, but Israel, because you struggled with God and with men and won."

Reflection

I watched as John slowly and painfully pulled himself out of the car and began shuffling with his two canes to the front door. After the home gathering I was determined to meet this gentleman who had clearly made a concerted effort to get to what was in essence a meeting designed to ask people for money. As I approached John he put one cane down and with an iron-like grip grasped my forearm saying, "Hey, preacher, are you the one who's leading this campaign?" Hmmm. Do I admit it or not? "Yes, John, I am helping your church with this campaign."

John continued, "Let me tell you something, preacher." Now I was truly worried! With his firm grip on my forearm and a twinkle in his eye John then said, "I am ninety-two years old and I spent most of last night wrestling with God and praying that prayer of yours, 'Lord, what do you want to do through me?' You see, preacher, I've already helped build two churches, and at ninety-two I can't tell you how excited I am to help build one more." John let go of my arm and slowly shuffled out to the car. I was stunned, almost speechless. John could have so easily said, "At ninety-two, I've done my share. I've done enough."

At ninety-two, I hope and pray I might spend the night like John wrestling with God, asking, "Lord, what would you do through me?" No matter our age or circumstance God always calls us to reach and stretch, to move out of our comfort zone. And as we wrestle with God, like Jacob and like John, we will indeed be blessed!

Have you ever wrestled with God in prayer? What happened? Have you been praying our prayer, "Lord, what do you want to do through me?" How has God begun answering your prayer?

Prayer

Oh God, give me the courage of Jacob and John to wrestle with you. Give me the courage and faith to ask, "Lord, what would you do through me?"

Day Thirteen

Scripture—Mark 9:43-47 CEB

If your hand causes you to fall into sin, chop it off. It's better for you to enter into life crippled than to go away with two hands into the fire of hell, which can't be put out. If your foot causes you to fall into sin, chop it off. It's better for you to enter life lame than to be thrown into hell with two feet. If your eye causes you to fall into sin, tear it out. It's better for you to enter God's kingdom with one eye than to be thrown into hell with two.

Reflection

What a positive and uplifting way to start the day!

Clearly, Jesus is not literally telling us to chop off a foot or pluck out an eye. He is, however, asking us to take inventory and consider what in our life separates us from God or prevents us from living as God wants us to live. Brian owns a private plane and frankly rarely flies it but Brian enjoys the satisfaction of knowing it's his. For the last eighteen months or so, Brian has had this nagging thought that he should perhaps sell the plane. Brian even began to get the strange thought that maybe God was the one doing the nagging.

For eighteen months, he wrestled with God and finally gave in. Not because having a plane was wrong but because for Brian it was a possession getting in the way of his relationship to God. Coincidently (if you believe in coincidences), this occurred in the midst of his church's capital campaign. For Brian there were no fireworks, no instant miracle, just a quiet act of obedience and generosity. Brian will be the first to tell you there may be another plane in his future but this plane will *not* get in the way of his relationship with God.

We all have those things that separate us from God. Like Brian, for some it might be "stuff." For others it might be pride, fear, a grudge, a refusal to forgive, a job, or a relationship. Spend a few minutes asking God, "What keeps me from loving you with all of my heart?"

Prayer

Oh God, thank for your divine patience. Thank you for loving me even as I stubbornly cling to my way and to my stuff. Help me to name it, and help me to surrender. Amen.

Day Fourteen

Scripture—Exodus 3:1-5 CEB

Moses was taking care of the flock for his father-in-law Jethro, Midian's priest. He led his flock out to the edge of the desert, and he came to God's mountain called Horeb. The LORD's messenger appeared to him in a flame of fire in the middle of a bush. Moses saw that the bush was in flames, but it didn't burn up. Then Moses said to himself, Let me check out this amazing sight and find out why the bush isn't burning up. When the LORD saw that he was coming to look, God called to him out of the bush, "Moses, Moses!" Moses said, "I'm here." Then the LORD said, "Don't come any closer! Take off your sandals, because you are standing on holy ground."

Reflection

I am enjoying my Lenten reading of the entire Bible, and I am just about finished with Exodus. I have been blessed in rereading some of the old familiar stories, like Moses and the burning bush.

Moses wasn't in church, wasn't on his knees in prayer, or wasn't even reading the Bible (of course he had no Bible to read); Moses was simply doing what he was supposed to be doing—tending his flock. In the midst of the normal everyday world, Moses encountered the burning bush. He heard the voice of God.

Now, how many of us have said, "I would do what God wants if he would give me a sign, give me a burning bush like Moses or write it across the sky"? In reading this passage I noticed something for the first time; *God* saw that Moses had stopped to look. God called to him from out of the bush. The surprise isn't in the burning bush but perhaps that Moses stopped and paid attention. He stopped! Think about this. Maybe the bush had been burning for days, months, or years and Moses was simply the first to stop and pay attention. How many potential saviors of Israel had just walked past the burning bush?

With my iPad by my side from morning till night; with my cell phone always present and on; how many times have I walked right past my own burning bush? We may not all get a burning bush, but I believe with all of my heart, God speaks to each of us throughout the day in many varied and ordinary ways. Today, take the time to stop and listen and with Moses say, "Yes, Lord, I'm right here. What do you want to do through me?"

Prayer

Oh God, forgive me for sometimes crowding you out of my busy schedule. Forgive me for being so preoccupied with stuff that I have failed to hear your voice. Help me, oh God, to pause, look, and listen. Help me, oh God, to see you, hear you, and have the courage to say, "Yes, I am right here." Amen.

Day Fifteen

Scipture—Matthew 19:23-26 CEB

Then Jesus said to his disciples, "I assure you that it will be very hard for a rich person to enter the kingdom of heaven. In fact, it's easier for a camel to squeeze through the eye of a needle than for a rich person to enter God's kingdom." When his disciples heard this, they were stunned. "Then who can be saved?" they asked. Jesus looked at them carefully and said, "It's impossible for human beings. But all things are possible for God."

Reflection

Why the heck does Jesus have to keep talking about this money thing, wealth and possessions? Life would be much nicer if Jesus was like most preachers and only talked about money once a year and then with an apology! So here we go again. As I read this I thought, *There's good news, there's bad news, and there's some more good news.*

Good news. I am rich. Yes, I am one of those and probably you are as well. There is a fun and revealing website called Am I Rich? (www.giving whatwecan.org/get-involved/how-rich-am-i). Plug in your income and it will tell you where you fall in the world rankings of wealth and income. Just for fun I plugged in $50,000. If you earn $50,000 with two people in your household, you are in the richest 3.9% of the population and your income is 21.6 times the global average. If you earn $200,000 with a household of two you are in the richest .1% of the world's population and your income is 86.3 times the global average. I am rich and in all likelihood most people reading this on their laptops, iPads, or smartphones are as well.

Bad news. I am rich and so are you. What did Jesus say to us? Jesus told his disciples, "I assure you that it will be very hard for a rich person to enter the kingdom of heaven. In fact, it's easier for a camel to squeeze through the eye of a needle than for a rich person to enter God's kingdom." How can this be? I still remember the first time a friend and pastor from Malawi, visited the United States. I asked him what he thought, and his reply was incredibly illuminating: "I know now why you Americans have such trouble with trust and faith in God. You don't need him. You have everything you need." (At least, what we think we need.)

Good news. So, what is the final piece of good news? Listen to the words of Jesus. The disciples were staggered. "Then who can be saved?" Jesus looked hard at them and said, "It's impossible for human beings. But all things are possible for God."

I can't do it, but God can. Can I trust? Can I have faith in something other than myself and my stuff?

Prayer

Dear God, I like having my stuff. I enjoy being rich. Forgive me for trusting in stuff other than you. Forgive me for thinking I have somehow earned all of this and deserve all of this. Fill my heart with gratitude, fill my heart with generosity, and in the end fill my heart with faith and trust only in you. Help me to trust that I might enter your kingdom. Amen.

Day Sixteen

Scripture—Leviticus 1:1-3 CEB

Then the LORD called to Moses and said to him from the meeting tent, Speak to the Israelites and say to them: When any of you present a livestock offering to the LORD, you can present it from either the herd or the flock. If the offering is an entirely burned offering from the herd, you must present a flawless male, bringing it to the meeting tent's entrance for its acceptance before the LORD.

Reflection

In reading the first chapter of Leviticus, one thing becomes instantly clear: God asks for our very best. And God asks for our best in a way that *all* can participate. If you had cattle or animals of any kind then you give the best of your herd. If you can't afford a cow or goat, then you can offer a bird, again the best. Can't do either cow, goat, or even a bird? Then there is grain, again, the first and the best.

Am I offering the best of my life and myself to God? I wonder. Sometimes I think I am offering God the leftovers of my life, and I am not talking only money. When I look at how I spend my time and attention, does God get only what is left after work, play, TV, and the other stuff I fill my day with?

What do my bank statements and credit card balances say about my offerings to God? When I get to the line of charitable contributions on my tax form, is God getting the best or just leftover scraps?

Today let each of us give our best as an offering to God.

Prayer

Oh God, you gave me the very best of yourself—your Son, Jesus. In joyful gratitude help me give you the very best of who I am and what I do. Amen.

Day Seventeen

Scripture—Romans 4:19-21 THE MESSAGE

Abraham didn't focus on his own impotence and say, "It's hopeless. This hundred-year-old body could never father a child." Nor did he survey Sarah's decades of infertility and give up. He didn't tiptoe around God's promise asking cautiously skeptical questions. He plunged into the promise and came up strong, ready for God, sure that God would make good on what he had said.

Reflection

Don't you just love the way THE MESSAGE translates these verses from Romans? Abraham did not tiptoe around God's promises...he plunged into the promises.

When it comes to getting into the water there are typically two kinds of people: those who plunge and those who tiptoe. Some just hate swimming in cold or even slightly chilly water and will tiptoe around the edge of a dock or along a beach. Then there are those brave or crazy souls who just stand back and with a shout run and take the plunge.

Sometimes the same is true for our faith and certainly for our giving. Sometimes we tiptoe around God and his promises, saying, "When I am a bit more comfortable, or when God makes things a bit more clear, when my return on investments is higher or my kids are done with school; then I will take the plunge of generosity." Unfortunately, we are never quite comfortable enough and things are never quite clear enough, we never seem to have enough; there is always something else to buy or invest in. The water is never quite warm enough and so we tiptoe and refuse to take the plunge.

Is God calling you to take the plunge of generosity? Have you perhaps been tiptoeing around the edges waiting until the water is just a bit warmer? Today, take the plunge! Claim the promise of Abraham who...

Didn't tiptoe around God's promise asking cautiously skeptical questions. He plunged into the promise and came up strong, ready for God, sure that God would make good on what he had said.

Prayer

God, I don't want to keep tiptoeing around you. Grant me the courage and the faith to take the plunge and leap into the water of your promises. Amen.

Day Eighteen

Scripture—Mark 10:21-22 CEB

Jesus looked at him carefully and loved him. He said, "You are lacking one thing. Go, sell what you own, and give the money to the poor. Then you will have treasure in heaven. And come, follow me." But the man was dismayed at this statement and went away saddened, because he had many possessions.

Reflection

Jesus looked him hard in the eye—and loved him! How often do we think Jesus really just loves the poor, the sick, and the downtrodden; of course Jesus loves the poor, the sick, and the downtrodden. But Jesus also has a very special place in his heart for those with resources, and yes, even those with wealth. Jesus wants those with wealth and resources to know him, love him, and follow him.

The real question being asked by Jesus is, "What do you love more than me?" For this young man the answer was clear: he loved stuff, money, and wealth more than Jesus. And so the young man turned away. And Jesus let him go. Can you imagine this scene in your head?

The man's face clouded over. This was the last thing he expected to hear, and he walked off with a heavy heart. He was holding on tight to a lot of things, and not about to let go.

Jesus looks us hard in the eye and with a heart overflowing with love asks, "What do you love more than me?" What are you holding on tight to and not about to let go? For a mother or father it could be children. For someone else it could be a parent or even a spouse. For others the answer may be found in a job, a career, a home. For many of us it may very well be our wealth and our stuff. Maybe it's the sense of pride and accomplishment that comes with having wealth and all the right "stuff." Maybe it's something very different like anger, bitterness, or an unwillingness to forgive that we refuse to let go. Jesus stands in front of you, looks you hard in the eye with love, and asks, "What do you love more than me?"

Prayer

God, I want to love you with all my heart. But there always seems to be stuff that gets in the way. Help me now today to let go, to release whatever my stuff is to you, your love, and your care. Amen.

Day Nineteen

Scripture—*2 Corinthians 8:3-4* CEB

I assure you that they gave what they could afford and even more than they could afford, and they did it voluntarily. They urgently begged us for the privilege of sharing in this service for the saints.

Reflection

One of the blessings of my job is occasionally I encounter one of the true saints of the church. Yesterday was such a day. While doing interviews in a very economically depressed area suffering from severe unemployment and all the problems associated with poverty, I met Miss Charlotte. Miss Charlotte came into the room with what appeared to be a slight limp and when she spoke slurred slightly certain words. My thought was, *She is suffering the aftereffects of a stroke.*

When we talked about her possibility of giving to a capital campaign she responded she was unable to because she had been the victim of a financial scam, had lost a large sum of money, and was forced into bankruptcy. But then her eyes lit up and a calm, beautiful smile came across her face as she then said, "But I haven't reduced my tithe. I asked the court permission to continue my giving to the church." Then she continued, "When I get out of bankruptcy in three years then I will be able to give something to the capital campaign." She ended our conversation by saying, "God has been so good to me. He has given me everything I have. He continues to care for me and I have everything I need because of him." Truly, I was in the presence of one of the true saints of God.

Prayer

Oh God, help me to trust you like Miss Charlotte. Forgive me for my lack of trust and my worries about the future. Give me a spirit of gratitude and a heart for generosity, even when it seems to make no sense. Amen.

Day Twenty

Scripture—1 Corinthians 3:18-19 CEB

Don't fool yourself. If some of you think they are worldly-wise, then they should become foolish so that they can become wise. This world's wisdom is foolishness to God. As it's written, He catches the wise in their cleverness.

Reflection

I like having answers. I don't like being a fool. After all, I am a consultant and I get paid for having answers. Being a fool in my line of work means I go hungry. But unless you are a comedian or a circus clown, the same is true for you. A teacher better be prepared with answers. A nurse or a doctor better have some idea of a diagnosis and treatment plan. A custodian better know how to clean a particular stain or wax a certain floor. Military officers had better not appear uncertain and unknowing; after all the lives of men and women are in their hands. My tax preparer and financial advisor better have answers to my questions or I will find someone else.

Don't fool yourself. Don't think that you can be wise merely by being up-to-date with the times. Be God's fool—that's the path to true wisdom. What the world calls smart, God calls stupid.

Two kids in college, a mortgage, and she already tithes, but she knows in her heart God wants her to give significantly to a mission project. Her financial advisor says it's foolish and not wise. She smiles and says, "I know."

Retirement is just around the corner and the house nearly paid off. Now is the time to start enjoying life. God calls him to go back to seminary and become a pastor. His best friend tells him he must be nuts. He smiles and says, "I know."

Her father who had abused her lay dying, alone and afraid. She hadn't spoken to him in years. She knew in her heart God was asking her to go and offer forgiveness. All of her friends and other family members said don't do it, he's not worth it. She smiles and says, "I know."

Don't fool yourself. Don't think that you can be wise merely by being up-to-date with the times. Be God's fool—that's the path to true wisdom. What the world calls smart, God calls stupid.

Prayer

Dear God, help me to have the courage to be foolish for you. Help me to trust in your wisdom and not my own. When you call, help me to say yes even when the world says no. Amen.

Day Twenty-One

Scripture—John 6:26-27 CEB

Jesus replied, "I assure you that you are looking for me not because you saw miraculous signs but because you ate all the food you wanted. Don't work for the food that doesn't last but for the food that endures for eternal life, which the Human One will give you. God the Father has confirmed him as his agent to give life."

Reflection

She is a very successful entrepreneur. She started and grew her business in a day and time when women typically either stayed home or worked in support roles. She made it to the top. Then cancer hit with a vengeance and she was told to get her life in order because she had only six months to live. All of a sudden, her success and all of her possessions and toys meant nothing to her. She read a book by John Ortberg that literally both changed and saved her life. Ortberg says that in the end life is like a game of Monopoly. We spend all our time and energy trying to acquire stuff: property, hotels, and money. All the while, we are trying to defeat everyone else and come in first. But in the end when the game is over, it all goes back into the box.

How much of our time and energy gets spent on pursuing those things in life that, in the words of Jesus, will never last? My home, my job, my toys—none of it will last. Even all the time I invest in running and staying in shape in the end won't really matter. But in the end when the game is over, it all goes back into the box. Think about that for a moment. In the end it all goes back into the box.

What are we doing of lasting importance with our time, our stuff, our money? Are we spending it all on stuff that goes back into the box or stuff that really matters—kingdom stuff?

Oh, and what happened to our successful businesswoman? She is still a success and still very much alive after five years, but she no longer plays Monopoly. She lives now with the heart of a generous, grateful servant. She lives and spends her time and money on kingdom stuff, not the stuff that simply goes back in the box. What about you?

Prayer

God, forgive me for spending so much of my time, energy, and resources on stuff that really doesn't matter. Help me today to do something that truly matters. I want to be part of building your kingdom. Amen.

Final Reflection

- After twenty-one days of walking on this journey of gratitude, prayer, and faith, how and where have you met Christ?

- How is your life different at the end of these twenty-one days?

- At the end of these twenty-one days, do you sense God calling you or leading you in a new direction?

To paraphrase Tom Peters, I pray these twenty-one days of devotions have led you on a novel journey to a place of surpassing importance. A place where you fully live out our generosity declaration:

We hold these truths to be self-evident that all people are created in the image of a loving, giving, and generous God. We believe real life, true liberty, and eternal joy are only realized when we live lives of abundant generosity and sacrificial love.

Let the Revolution begin and may it begin with me, oh Lord.

CPSIA information can be obtained
at www.ICGtesting.com
Printed in the USA
LVOW04s0920250116

471923LV00001B/1/P